Arguably the best athlete in Australia, P
distinction of having represented Austr
soccer World Cups.

Perry became the youngest Australian
international cricket when she made he
the Rose Bowl Series in Darwin in July
birthday.

She went on to make her domestic debut in the 2007-08 Women's
National Cricket League season, taking 2-29 from 10 overs in her
first match.

Since her national debut, Perry has become a regular fixture for the
Southern Stars, playing in the 2009 ICC Women's World Cup and
the ICC Women's World Twenty20 in the same year.

Leading Australia's bowling attack, Perry played a crucial role in the
ICC Women's World Twenty20 Final in the West Indies in 2010. The
match came down to the wire, with New Zealand requiring five runs
off the last ball to claim the title. Under immense pressure, Perry
bowled the final ball of the tournament, which New Zealand's
Sophie Devine struck straight off the bat.

The talented footballer stuck out her boot to deflect the ball to Lisa
Sthalekar at mid-on, securing the trophy for Australia. Perry's figures
of 3-18 in the final saw her take home the Player of the Match
award.

Perry featured prominently in Australia's three-peat of World T20
victories, also sealing her spot in the Team of the Tournament in
2012 and 2014.

In 2013, Perry played a key role in Australia claiming the ICC
Women's World Cup in India in 2013, despite suffering an ankle
injury. She finished with 3-19 in the final, claiming the scalps of the
West Indies' top three batters.

Perry was named player of the series in Australia's Ashes triumph
over England in 2015 and captained the Sydney Sixers in WBBL|01.

In 2018, Perry was an integral part of the Australian Women's cricket
team which went all the way to win a fourth ICC World T20
championship.

During the 2018 ICC Women's World T20 tournament in the West
Indies, Perry became the first cricketer for Australia, male or female,
to play 100 Twenty20 International matches. In the final of the same
tournament, she became the first cricketer for Australia, male or
female, to take 100 wickets in Twenty20 International matches.

PERSPECTIVE

ELLYSE

PERSPECTIVE

PERRY

Harper
Collins

PERSPECTIVE.

DEDICATION

Dedicated to finding joy and fulfilment
in the process — and incredible people
to share it with

CON T

ENTS

PERSP

ADVEN

MY NOT

COURA

DREAM

INDEPE

BELIEF

PERSPECTIVE

he word 'perspective' means a lot to me and it's been something that I've thought more and more about in the last few years.

What are the important things that you know make the experience special? What are the things that motivate you? What are the things that give you joy? The things that challenge you but ultimately make you a better person? Most importantly, who are the people whose unwavering help and support you couldn't go without?

PERSPECTIVE IS ABOUT SITTING BACK FROM THE WORLD YOU'RE INVOLVED IN AND EVALUATING WHAT IT MEANS TO YOU.

My goal in writing this book has been twofold: 1) I've tried to provide my perspective on what it is to be an elite athlete, including the things and habits that I've adopted to help me along the way; and 2) what the things are that truly matter in the scheme of life.

First up, I want to be really clear in saying that by no means is this intended to be a catalogue of advice-giving or a self-help book. It would be incredibly naive and arrogant of me to think that I have the answers. I definitely do not, and I've still got a lot to learn. But I do want to share some of the experiences I've had over ten years of playing top-level sport, as well as some of the things that were really impactful in my childhood.

It's my hope that you find this vaguely interesting, and if you're able to take something away from it, then I would be ecstatic. At the very least, I hope it gives you some idea of just how much incredible help and support I have had from so many people.

My perspective has also changed a lot along the way, as I'm sure everyone's does across the course of time. For me, the change has come from various experiences, some incredible people influencing the way I think, and just growing up in general. While there are things that I wish I had learned earlier, I don't think there is anything I would change. All of it has been an incredible journey, one that I can never truly understand why I've been afforded the opportunity to live out.

I've had experiences and learned various things along the way that have added to my knowledge or influenced my opinions. But I'm still learning – some days I get things right and feel on top of the world, other days I get things totally wrong and learn a lot as a result. That's the point, though, I suppose. It's not about the great days, the achievements, the medals. It's about the process.

To be honest, right now I'm sitting on a train and pondering how, in so many ways, it doesn't feel right that I have the opportunity to write a book. I have long grappled with the whole notion of athletes being role models, and also the bizarre fact that because I'm good at hurling a leather ball down twenty-two yards of turf, and at times hitting that same ball off the turf and into the field, why I'm entitled to this platform to tell you my story and what I think about various subject matter. Sure, to some extent, I'm an expert on cricket by virture of playing this sport for a living and it's what I do most days of the week. But beyond that, I'm just trying to figure out the world like everyone else.

IT'S ABOUT THE **WEALTH OF EXPERIENCE** AND THE **VALUE THAT STICKING AT SOMETHING,** TRYING AS HARD AS YOU CAN **TO BE THE BEST YOU CAN,** THAT ADDS TO YOUR LIFE.

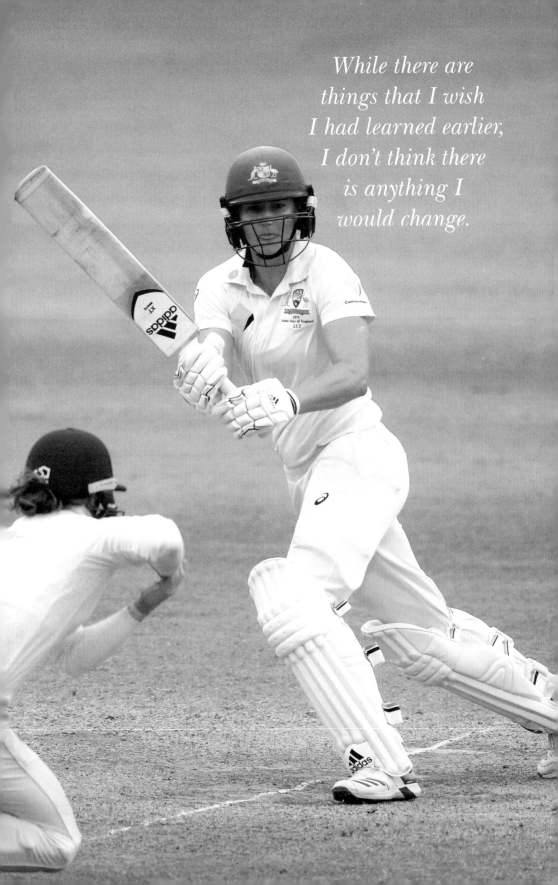

While there are things that I wish I had learned earlier, I don't think there is anything I would change.

Sport for me, and specifically cricket these days, is the avenue I've found to provide personal meaning and purpose, without it defining me. But I think this is equally applicable to so many other professions or pursuits. When I'm a washed-up has-been with a few sore joints, I really hope that I can find the same purpose and excitement in other areas.

It's an extreme pleasure and privilege to be able to share my story with you. I want to make the most of this incredible opportunity. I want this book to be enjoyable. I want this book to explain what drives me, what motivates me, what inspires me, what makes me want to keep evolving and improving as an athlete and a human being. But I really don't want it to be preachy.

We're all different. We all want different things. We all have different interests and passions and hobbies and careers. We all have different personalities – that's the beauty of it.

If two of us want the same thing, we're probably going to walk two different roads to get there.

ne coach has had a profound effect on me, Tom Sermanni. He was the Matildas coach for a number of years, universally loved by everyone, staff and players alike. Amazing fellow. A Scotsman. He just had an incredible disposition and way of relating to everyone in the team. I remember one time when everyone was together at a Matildas camp and players were coming in and out at different times and there was a bit of disharmony around that. Why doesn't she have to be here? Stuff like that.

Tommy sat everyone down and said: 'I want you all to know, I will always treat you fairly. All of you. I will always be

honest with you. I will always be up-front with you because that's how I think a team works best. Not everyone is going to be happy all of the time. But if I'm honest with you, and if you're honest with me, and if we're all honest with each other, we can make it work. But I cannot treat you all the same. You're all different. You have different circumstances, different personalities, different approaches. You all sit differently within this group.'

I always remembered that. It was the most honest and fair assessment I'd ever heard from a coach. Tommy genuinely lived that out, and he had the challenge of bringing it all together for the team. Point being, what has worked for me may not work for you. And what has worked for you may not work for me. But I like the idea of sharing ideas and then plucking out the things that sound right.

WE WERE **ENCOURAGED TO BE INDIVIDUALS** WITH **UNIQUE QUALITIES.**

Tommy had this wonderful ability to find the funny or ridiculous side to situations, even when he was being serious. You still understood he was being serious, but he'd give us a one-liner that would lighten the mood just the right amount. It probably suited me because I've done a lot of stupid things on the field, accidentally, and I guess I knew he wasn't going to give me a hard time about it. The delivery of his messages was brilliant.

I vividly remember the time when Tommy played an April Fools' joke on the entire squad, back in 2011. We had been in camp for a while at the AIS, in Canberra, a few months out from the start of the FIFA World Cup coming up later in the year in Germany. Tommy pulled the team in as a group on the field just before the start of training. Normally, we only ever had a chat in the change rooms before we headed out onto the field, and once we were on the field we would crack on with getting warmed up, etc. But at this session Tommy had brought down the director of the AIS, essentially one of his bosses, and asked us to stop warm-up and gather around.

What ensued was a four- or five-minute explanation about how Tommy had decided to take a job in Japan working with one of their J-League teams, effective immediately and leaving us high and dry without a coach for the World Cup in a few months' time. The director of the AIS then stepped in to explain that they would begin searching to find a suitable replacement for us.

I still remember looking around the circle at all the players as this was unfolding – there were very few dry eyes in the team. People were genuinely devastated, angry and then shocked at the thought of losing Tommy. Someone put there hand up at the end of the formalities and choked through a question of, 'But how could you do this to us?' A wry smile crossed Tommy's face, and then he muttered quietly in his thick Scottish accent, 'April Fools'. People absolutely lost it. Tommy hardly flinched, took a sip of tea and headed back to his little office to do the crossword, while we tried to regain composure and finish warming up.

When I was younger, I read Susie O'Neill's book *Choose to Win*. She's a hero of mine – for what she's achieved as an athlete and, equally, the way she's done it. I've always kept that book, called on it, drawn from it. I can tell you the chapter names: Pain. Self-doubt. Fair Play. Perseverance. Crossroads. Belief. Focus. Delivering. Gold. Reward. I can relate to all the categories, we all can. It doesn't matter what we're striving for, those areas confront us all.

I've been given so much advice over the years. Some of it has been invaluable. Some of it not so much. Half the trick is to understand yourself well enough to know what suits you and what doesn't.

Hopefully, as you read this, I am able to convey a little about my beliefs and the parts of my journey so far that have shaped a lot of the way I see the world. I'm certainly not attempting to convey the meaning of life, though. I haven't been on this earth long enough to have even the slightest clue of what that may be. I have a few strengths, but my weaknesses far outweigh these. There are things that I'm completely hopeless at – I can't sing, I can't dance and I'd love to be able to play a musical instrument well. I'm shy, and public speaking is probably one of my biggest phobias. I also have an incredible ability to spill most things I'm attempting to eat.

But I've found certain things I love to do. I don't know if I love them because I'm good at them, or if I'm good at them because I love them. A bit of both. maybe?

If there's one little snippet in this book that helps you in any way, I'll be thrilled. Whether you're a fan of sport or not, whether you're a twelve-year-old picking up the book or a fifty-year-old, I'm just going to talk about the concepts I've found useful. I hope there's some positivity to be found in here. The more positive influences in the world, the better. We're all on our own journeys and we all have our own stories to tell.

So, here's mine.

THE MORE POSITIVE INFLUENCES IN THE WORLD, THE BETTER.

HALF THE TRICK IS TO **UNDERSTAND YOURSELF** WELL ENOUGH TO **KNOW WHAT SUITS YOU** AND WHAT DOESN'T.

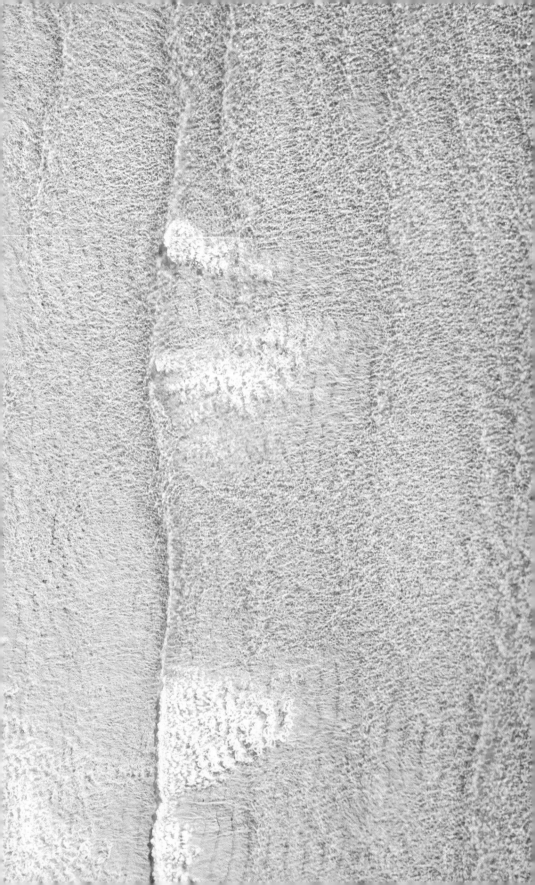

MY NOTEBOOK

MY NOTEBOOK

have had a notebook for as long as I can remember. I take it everywhere. I'm the only one who reads it. It's pretty eclectic in there and probably wouldn't make much sense to others. Inside are all sorts of thoughts and observations and quotes that I love. The quotes are nice little reminders of the things that are important to mc.

THOUGHTS BECOME MORE REAL WHEN THEY ARE WRITTEN DOWN. AND DREAMS. AND HOPES.

I've always found writing cathartic. I like the simplicity of it. No digital pop-up pages, just real pages, none of the distractions we get on electronic devices. When I get a bit of quiet time, I like having something with me to write in. I love that you can write anywhere, at any time – in a café, on a plane, at home, early in the morning, late at night.

There are a lot of things in my notebook that I don't revisit. Fleeting things that I want to get out at the time but once they're out, they're gone for good. But there are a few scribbles I come back to regularly.

have written plenty of cricket notes before a game. I always write them on the morning of a match and, really, they all look the same! There are notes reviewing a match or team notes on opposition players and thoughts on other sport-related things like goals, training ideas and programs, high performance and team dynamics, which I'm quite passionate about.

FINAL V. ENGLAND, ICCWT20   24TH, NOVEMBER 2018

☐ BAT
• assess conditions & situation as game goes & have a clear plan
  of approach
• Basics are best - good weight towards the ball, play late, use
                    feet.
• v. spin: decisive fwd & back with foot work
          get good energy, momentum & shape through the ball when
          going big
          use depth of crease & assess to horizontal v. vertical shots
• Let the ball come, use depth of crease & adjust to slower balls
• Run hard

☐ BOWL
• aggressive straight & powerful approach
• work on foot alignment & strong front shoulder
• hard lengths, pick up batter cues & movement
• slower ball - bowl it & keep running!
• Stay ahead of the batter

☐ FIELD
• athletic, agile, alert
• do the hard yards early under the ball
• tactically aware
• supportive
• 100% hard throws
        CONFIDENCE, BELIEF, DETERMINATION, RESILIENCE

Right now, I'm writing about the things I want to write about in this book. If that makes sense.

If I come across any quotes that I like, or quotes I think are relevant to any aspect of my life, I'll put them down as well.

I also write about the really important stuff: food, coffee, travel, music, reading.

────

ne of the favourite quotes in my notebook is this Michael Jordan take on success and failure. The notion that, ultimately, you become more successful because of how many times you fail:

'I'VE MISSED MORE THAN 9,000 SHOTS IN MY CAREER. I'VE LOST ALMOST 300 GAMES. TWENTY-SIX TIMES I'VE BEEN TRUSTED TO TAKE THE GAME-WINNING SHOT AND MISSED. I'VE FAILED OVER AND OVER AND OVER AGAIN IN MY LIFE. AND THAT IS WHY I SUCCEED.'

– MICHAEL JORDAN

There's one quote I love above all others – it's from Don Bradman.

In so many ways, these words represent Bradman and everything he was as a cricketer and as a person. There is no sportsperson in the history of Australian sport who's had as great an impact on our country.

I think this is because Bradman is admired for so many things, not least his batting average of 99.94, but also because of his exceptional standing as a human being. He's admired for his humility, his intellect, his tremendous talent at many things and his dedication to his family.

Bradman's words are so powerful and challenging. Although I never saw him play, these words feel like they are bigger and more beautiful than anything he did on a cricket field.

Bradman's words remind me of who I want to be, who I wish I could be, who I'm trying to be, who I'm hoping to be as time goes on.

" When considering the stature of an
athlete, or for that matter, any person,
I set great store in certain qualities
which I believe to be essential in
addition to skill. They are that
a person conducts his or her life
with dignity, with integrity, courage
& perhaps most of all, with modesty.
These virtues are totally compatible
with pride, ambition & competitiveness.
Hard work & dedication remain essential
for all individuals who must embrace,
with equal fervor, opportunity &
responsibility."

Donald Bradman.

BELIEF

This word means everything to me. There's a song I listen to that describes belief as a beautiful armour. As something that makes anything possible. What can take us to where we want to go? Belief can. What can give us the confidence and strength we need? Belief can. I've played it on the way to matches for as long as I can remember. That one word – belief – grabs me.

It started when I was playing soccer for Australia. We were away with the Matildas in Vietnam. We were on our way to the stadium and I had my iPod on shuffle and this song came on. The chorus just hit me.

THE WHOLE NOTION OF BELIEF, FOR ME, IS TO HAVE A DEEP-SEATED CONFIDENCE IN YOURSELF.

Belief isn't expressed arrogantly. It's not about drawing attention to yourself or showing off or rubbing other people's faces in it when you win.

Belief is what is inside you.

Belief doesn't depend on what a scoreboard says. Belief doesn't disappear because you're nervous or you're in a form slump. Confidence can come and go, and it definitely has for me over the years, but belief is more important.

It's a genuine belief in your ability at a really, really deep level. It's so deep that you don't have to talk about it, you don't have to show it to anyone else, you don't have to prove it to anyone else.

There's only one person who needs to know it's there.

Me.

Belief doesn't sit on the surface. Belief is what gets you through the toughest moments. You can probably fake confidence, but you can't fake belief. I often think that you can intuitively tell when someone has belief. It's in the way they carry themselves, the way they respond to every little situation, this look in their eyes that says I know I can do this. Once you have belief, you're never really beaten.

You may lose a match or make a duck or bowl rubbish and it may not be your particular day, but if you have belief you know it will swing your way again, soon. Confidence can be fleeting. Real belief is always there. I think of the difference between belief and confidence like the difference between peace and happiness. Peace is deep and meaningful and immovable. Happiness is one of the things that stems from it, but you know those highs aren't always going to last. Belief lasts.

If one thing has served me especially well, it's a fundamental belief in myself as an athlete. I can be against people who are playing the best soccer or cricket in the world, but I've found the core belief that tells me I can play it with them.

When you believe you can, you really can.

onfidence goes up and down. It depends on circumstance and form and feel. Some days, it just doesn't feel right. You're not hitting the ball in the way you're used to. Your run-up doesn't feel like it has the right rhythm. There's no real reason for it. You're not doing anything too differently from the day before, but you're less confident. If the belief is still there, that's all you're going to need. You just have to know it's in there somewhere. I may not be confident about something at a certain moment, but I still have the belief that I can be good at it.

BELIEF IS WHAT STOPS ME FROM GIVING UP.

Waiting on the sidelines as the next person to bat, you can be sitting there and absolutely packing it with nerves if someone is bowling particularly well or the pitch is difficult that day. But, for some reason, I've never wanted to run from that. I've never gone, 'I wish I didn't have to go out there'. I've always wanted to have a go at it. There's no point being there if you're not going to do it properly. Even when it's really tough, I still believe I can do it. It doesn't mean I will actually do it! But belief can make you stubborn. Sometimes you've just got to get stubborn with yourself and walk into something you may be a bit afraid of.

What can make you push yourself when you're not sure if you're up to it? Belief can. Sometimes you're conscious of the belief you have in yourself, and other times it just sits there as the foundation to everything you are doing, without you even realising it.

The great thing about belief is that it doesn't discriminate; it's there in good times, and in bad times.

Any time. Any place. Every time. Every place.

Belief has underpinned everything I've ever done.

DREAM

wasn't the kind of kid who dreamed of what they wanted to be when they grew up. I just dreamed of the things that were right in front of me. I did the things I enjoyed and loved without making any grand plans about where they might lead. Dreams don't have to be big dreams. They can be small dreams that, when strung together, get bigger and bigger until there's a huge one at the end and you're thinking, 'I could never have even imagined this!' I just always had a go at stuff.

ONE OF THE **MOST VALUABLE THINGS IN MY LIFE** HAS BEEN **SAYING 'YES' TO GIVING SOMETHING A GO.** SAYING 'YES' TO THE CHALLENGES.

I never really had any trepidation about putting myself into situations that may have been uncomfortable. I've been anxious and scared and nervous and all those things, but I know when those feelings come along they prove what I'm doing means something to me.

I like the thought of being fearless. I want to try to be bold. Something in me kicks in that over-rides the negativity and beats it.

The most nervous I've ever been in sport has been around school athletics carnivals. I absolutely hated them! I can still remember being completely petrified. I wasn't great at athletics. I wasn't trying to live up to any expectations, and I wasn't scared about losing – what I was nervous about was being completely alone in an individual sport. That's always been scary to me. In all the games I've played for Australia in cricket and soccer, I've never felt as nervous as I did before those athletics carnivals.

I didn't bomb out. I did okay at those carnivals. But I hated the lot of it. I hated waking up on the morning of the event. I hated going to the event. I remember standing there, feeling isolated and alone. I didn't have teammates. I wasn't playing with people. We were all trying to beat each other. When it's just you by yourself, you've only got yourself to satisfy or let down.

If you win by yourself, it doesn't feel as good. And if you lose by yourself, it definitely doesn't feel as good because there is no one to share the disappointment with, or to help you pick up your bottom lip and realise that what you're doing is playing a game, and no matter how big that game was in your little bubble, in the grand scheme of life it's a blip on the radar. As I've grown older, and experienced many different things in team environments, the more I've realised that perhaps your greatest responsibility is to do the right thing by the other people. Not just the people in your team, but also the opposition, the officials and, maybe most importantly, the people who decide you are worthy of their attention and turn up to watch you play of their own accord.

In isolation, doing the right thing by someone else may not seem like a massive deal, and I would be absolutely lying if I didn't say that at times I've acted selfishly – I think that's an ingrained habit in athletes by the nature of our profession. But cumulatively, the effect that a team or individual athlete can have by making others feel good is pretty incredible, and maybe the most important (and rewarding) role that our sporting teams play in society.

played a bit of tennis when I was younger, but it was the same thing – you're massively on your own. When you're competing on your own, who's in your corner? No one. I want people in my corner, and I want to be in the corner of the people I'm with.

My primary school athletics carnivals were held at the local Cherrybrook oval in Sydney's northwest suburbs. But my high school carnivals were at Homebush, where the Sydney Olympics were held, so they were a little fancier and even more intimidating. Cherrybrook had the grass track and Homebush had the tartan track.

I've never been particularly quick as a runner. I'm okay, but not super quick. I ended up getting pushed into the hurdles at high school because not many other girls liked jumping them. By the end of high school, hurdles was my event. I wouldn't call it my pet event – you're meant to love your pets. The funny thing is, it wasn't the actual hurdles that scared me. A lot of people are terrified of tripping on a hurdle and getting injured. I think because as a kid I was always down at the park – jumping off things, taking risks, getting bumps and bruises, mucking around with climbing trees and doing jumps on my bike, skateboarding, roller-blading, all those things. Having a sense of danger about it probably took my mind off the fact I was on my own.

Hurdles? Let's jump! I didn't have any issue with running or hurdling over something. I enjoyed it more than a normal running race because there was more to it. You needed some extra coordination, which gave me a slight, very slight, fighter's chance. I'd feel sick with nerves, but I'd always do it. You just get yourself to the start line and see what happens.

I value being uncomfortable and being in situations where it's not all roses. I think that concept has helped me a lot. That's where you get your adrenaline from, and you start to learn to enjoy it. When it ends well, the feeling is more euphoric because you didn't know if you could do it at all.

If I know I can do something, and then I do it, so what? What have I proved about myself? Not much.

DOING **SOMETHING THAT SCARES ME A BIT,** THAT'S WHAT **INSPIRES ME.**

I've lived a few dreams. Having the opportunity to represent my country in two sports that I absolutely love, and to have been a part of it during an era of such incredible progress, was impossible to imagine when I started out. I think, sometimes, all the little dreams you have, the ones you have day to day, can lead to a large, unfathomable dream without you realising what's happening.

A dream has to be realistic. It has to be something you can actually do.

I dream of being a musician and playing live shows and having people weep because my songs mean so much to them. But that's not a real dream, because I'm lucky to play 'Frère Jacques' on a school recorder, let alone play anything else. I'm lucky to sing without breaking the nearest window pane.

Dreams evolve naturally. You don't have to have your life mapped out when you're fifteen years old. But once you've walked up to the starting line in a lot of different things, and once you've found the thing or things that you're naturally passionate about, you won't be able to help dreaming. And that's when your life really begins.

You might end up living a dream that's bigger and better than any of the dreams you've had along the way.

DREAM

ROAM

am one hundred per cent certain there are many positives to growing up outdoors. Let me tell you about my childhood. What I most remember is this: being out and about, roaming the neighbourhood finding random things to do and see. Just being a kid.

I have an older brother named Damien, who we all call Dee. He's three years older than me. I was his shadow every day after school. We'd roam the neighbourhood until it got dark – and after dark a lot of times. It was the same on weekends. We didn't have mobile phones or the internet or screens to swipe or photos to post or any of the things that tempt kids these days to stay inside.

If my brother and I wanted to play on PlayStation, we'd have to get on our bikes and ride for half an hour to a friend's house who had it.

Without electronic devices, we used to make our own fun. Bushwalking. Riding bikes – whatever would get us there faster. You learn so much about yourself by going out and doing that stuff. Putting yourself in random situations – not dangerous or risky ones, just fun – going looking for them. Telling each other, 'I can't believe what happened!'

From a creativity point of view, what can kids do today to let their imaginations run wild?

I'm grateful that when I was a kid ways to enjoy myself weren't put in my lap. I had to go out and find them. I think it makes you independent and resourceful and self-aware. I wanted to find as many adventures as I could. As a kid, you don't have to travel the world to have an adventure – if your imagination is big enough, you can have one in your local park. Making your own fun was the best. It still is.

These days, I can get sucked into Netflix as much as anyone, but when I re-emerge I usually think, 'Well, there's two hours of my life I'll never get back.'

And perhaps at the time, what I really needed to do was switch off and watch a screen for a few hours. I'm certainly no Gandhi, I can't meditate for hours and feel content. But I do think it's easy to get sucked in to a vortex of having other people imagine for you. There's a balance to be found there and, in my opinion, the scales have been tipped a little too unevenly in technology's favour.

AS A KID, YOU
DON'T HAVE
TO TRAVEL THE
WORLD TO HAVE
AN ADVENTURE –
IF YOUR
IMAGINATION IS
BIG ENOUGH,
YOU CAN HAVE
ONE IN YOUR
LOCAL PARK.

grew up on the north shore of Sydney in houses that backed onto the bush. My brother and I would just disappear into there. That was our wonderland. There was nothing particularly wonderful about it – trees and dirt tracks.

WE WERE FREE TO MAKE IT WHATEVER WE WANTED. OUR PLACE FOR ADVENTURES.

You see a branch up a tree and wonder if you can climb up there. Then you realise, wow, you can! You see a jump and wonder if you can make it. Wow, you did! It's such a great way to build confidence.

My brother pushed me to do things I was scared of. The thrill of doing those things – it gets to the stage where being scared of it is the best reason of all to want to do it. Dee and I got this wonder from being able to do things we didn't know we could do. It makes you think you might be able to do anything if you're brave enough to give it a try. We climbed a lot of trees. Rode a lot of bikes. Threw a lot of rocks. Played hide-and-seek in the bush. Built cubby-houses. It was more fun than sitting inside and watching TV. If a friend had a backyard swimming pool, sometimes we'd go there. It didn't matter how far we had to go, that was part of the adventure. We'd go to the milk bar and buy a bunch of lollies. Frogs were always my first choice, but I didn't discriminate – I was a lolly fiend.

We'd just keep moving, throwing ourselves into one thing and then thinking, 'Okay, what's next?'

Not that roaming didn't go without its hitches. I got my share of bumps and bruises, and scratches – but it was worth it. Even the fights that normally ensued with my brother after a stack never lasted that long. We used to skateboard and do the luge down our steep driveway.

Sometimes, when I was feeling daring, I'd chuck my rollerblades on and traverse down the driveway like a slalom skier heading down a mountain. I remember being on my blades one day at the top of our driveway on the flat

part. I was going through my rugby league collector cards (the Parramatta Eels and Mark Tookey were favourites) and gloating to Dee about how cool all the ones I had collected were. I must have really been getting on his nerves, because he grabbed the cards out of my hands and threw them down the driveway. Without thinking, I took off after them, and then mid-slope I realised exactly where I was and what I was doing and freaked out. I got the speed wobbles, stacked it and ended up sliding the rest of the distance down the driveway on my bare legs. I still wince at the thought of Mum picking the gravel out of my legs in the bath afterwards.

Dee was really good at mountain bike riding. One day I was following him when he went off a ledge. It was a complete drop, a long way down onto some grass. I was right behind him, saw him do it and pulled up after he flew off.

My brother: 'Have a crack!'

Me: 'No thanks!'

My brother: 'Go on! You can do it. Just make sure you get a bit of speed and keep going fast.'

Of course, I went in way too cautiously, tumbled over the handlebars and then over the ledge. But he was right about one thing: it was good to have a crack.

IT MAKES YOU THINK **YOU MIGHT BE ABLE TO DO** ANYTHING IF YOU'RE **BRAVE ENOUGH TO GIVE IT A TRY.**

PLAY

played quite a lot of tennis when I was younger. And touch football. And so many other sports. Mum and Dad were sporty, so Dad taught me to catch and throw and hit and whatever else popped up in the backyard.

Soccer and cricket started the same year for me – soccer all winter and cricket all summer – and there weren't any girls' teams. I was a massive tomboy and absolutely loved playing in the boys' teams. Every now and then other girls might come along and play but, all in all, it was boys. I was lucky that all the guys in my team were brilliant about having me there. They're still some of my best friends now. But every once in a while, I'd rock up to a game and when the opposition saw me I'd hear them say: 'We're going to win easily today, they've got a girl in their team, they can't be any good and we know she won't be any good!'

That was fine. It wasn't enjoyable to hear, but it didn't bother me, either. It didn't make me want to prove them all wrong – that wasn't why I was playing. I just wanted to be involved in a game of cricket. That was it.

It'll sound silly but to me it was just, why shouldn't I be playing? Whatever you think of me, it doesn't really matter. I wasn't trying to impress anyone or prove myself. I knew I was good enough to play, so there was no reason not to. I just wanted to have some fun and be challenged and see if I was any good on the day.

IT'S ABSOLUTELY BRILLIANT THAT TODAY THERE ARE SO MANY ALL-GIRL COMPETITIONS IN CRICKET AND SOCCER.

The increase in the number of girls playing both sports has been nothing short of phenomenal. Those kinds of numbers weren't the case when I began playing and, from a theory point of view, I really think that if girls are comfortable playing in mixed teams at that age, when body size and

I WAS **A MASSIVE TOMBOY** AND **ABSOLUTELY LOVED PLAYING** IN THE **BOYS' TEAMS.**

strength isn't a factor, then it's a great experience. For both sexes, it provides a cool chance for social interaction that's based around an activity everyone loves doing. And you learn different ways to play in a competitive environment.

I will always remember my first ever game of soccer, for the Beecroft Wombats Under-7s side. Actually, that's not quite correct, I don't remember the game at all. But I do remember being totally mortified and embarrassed. (Mum will kill me for writing about this story.) I can't recall the specific circumstances, but somehow I ended up getting out of the car at the first game with long grey school socks wedged into my brand new soccer boots, covering my shin pads and pulled up to my knees. I'd thought nothing of it until I was approaching my new teammates and saw them all looking at me funny. I then looked down at their legs, all of them with these pristine white socks with blue stripes covering their shin pads.

I'm pretty sure it took some convincing to coax me out from hiding behind the toilet block, to go onto the field. Needless to say, I wore the proper socks the next week.

I JUST WANTED TO **HAVE SOME FUN** AND **BE CHALLENGED** AND **SEE IF I WAS ANY GOOD** ON THE DAY.

RESILIENCE

he idea of resilience in this chapter is not the notion of getting through something really horrible that has happened to you.

I have been very fortunate to have not been in those circumstances and so I wouldn't dare to try and relate to something on that level.

RESILIENCE, FOR ME, IS MORE THE ACCEPTANCE THAT NOT EVERYTHING CAN HAPPEN PERFECTLY, OFTEN FAR FROM IT, AND THAT CHALLENGES ARE A GOOD THING, PARTICULARLY IN SPORT.

It's not always as easy as that. If problems turn up, it's natural to think, why now? Why me? Things would be so much better without this.

Resilience is really all about your response. Instead of thinking something is a lost cause, it's telling yourself, 'No one can, or should, work harder for me than me', so the solution is to give it your all and not give up.

If you need something to be fixed, there's going to a be a means to fix it out there, somewhere. You just have to be motivated enough to go looking for it, and content enough with the fact it may take some time and you might have to do a lot of the heavy lifting yourself.

It's not necessarily about finding answers to big problems all the time either. It's also about turning up each day and adjusting to things that don't go perfectly to plan. In my opinion, the most resilient athletes are the ones you often don't even realise are dealing with and fixing problems all the time – with barely a chink in their armour, they adjust and get on with things, knowing that ultimately they'll be better for it.

s a kid, purely through having some level of natural coordination and by being interested in sport, I was fortunate that I ended up being successful in most of the junior cricket and soccer that I played. There certainly weren't any repercussions if you played a poor game or didn't quite apply yourself. In many, many ways, that's a great aspect of kids playing sport.

KIDS SHOULD JUST BE ABLE TO PLAY AND ENJOY IT FOR WHAT IT IS AND FEEL LIKE THEY ARE NOT PLAYING FOR ANY REASON OTHER THAN TO HAVE FUN.

The one thing that playing youth sport doesn't prepare you for, though, is that, when you start playing at a senior level, expectations and the responsibility that people place on you to perform change quite significantly. I don't mean that as a negative thing; elite sport by its very nature is competitive and, at times, demanding. It's what leads to people pushing themselves to limits they probably didn't know they were capable of, and it's what creates some of the greatest stories of triumph we bear witness to.

In extraordinary circumstances, those stories become woven into our culture, and, in the case of someone like Cathy Freeman winning the gold medal at the 2000 Sydney Olympics, they have the ability to lift an entire nation. I was only nine years old at the time, but I will never, ever forget that image of her crossing the finish line in the full body suit she wore with the green hood. I don't think any Australian will ever forget that.

Resilience in sport means that you have to take responsibility for yourself, your performance, your preparation and, in a broader sense, what it is that you want to be your impact on the sport and the people you play and work alongside. I think we all have visions of how things will pan out – the best case scenarios and smooth sailing circumstances that lead to success. The percentage of times things actually play out like that, though, would be very low, and probably very boring if it did go that way too.

RESILIENCE

---

am cautious in writing about this because, in so many ways, I feel like the journey and experiences I've had have been, in comparison to many other people, a very fortunate and hassle-free ride. I think the one thing I have deliberately and actively sought to do is surround myself with people who believe in me, want to support and help me in any way they can, and have an understanding of what my aspirations are and want to encourage me to go for them.

That's not to say that I've surrounded myself with 'yes' people, but I have deliberately tried to be quite naive and, perhaps, blissfully aloof to anyone or any circumstances that are negative towards my goals. This probably reads as though I have been quite selfish in my way of thinking and have not wanted to listen to criticism. But I believe there is a clear difference between constructive feedback, with a

RESILIENCE IN SPORT MEANS THAT YOU HAVE TO TAKE RESPONSIBILITY FOR YOURSELF, YOUR PERFORMANCE, YOUR PREPARATION AND, IN A BROADER SENSE, WHAT IT IS THAT YOU WANT TO BE YOUR IMPACT ON THE SPORT AND THE PEOPLE YOU PLAY AND WORK ALONGSIDE.

goal to making you better, and the kind of criticism that is solely about expressing a dislike for who you are and what you are doing.

I have always had two strong driving factors in chasing my dreams. The first is that I have never wanted to allow other people to tell me what I'm capable of. That has to be entirely up to me to decide and figure out. The other is that I have one chance to make the most of the incredible opportunities I've been given, and that sport, in the grand scheme of life, lasts only a short period of time. I don't want to look back and wish I had tried harder or wish that I hadn't shied away from something because people wanted to tell me I couldn't and I listened to them, even though I thought I could.

airly predictably, maybe the greatest and best challenge I had was when I was playing both cricket and soccer. I haven't played soccer for nearly five years now, and in a lot of ways it feels like a whole lifetime ago. It certainly feels like a whole other career ago. So much has changed in those five years – the entire female sporting landscape has developed, evolved and made amazing progress. A lot of that development is what precipitated me to play just cricket. It got to a point where, feasibly, it was almost impossible to play both sports because of the time demands becoming greater and greater. Very poignantly, the chance to be a full-time paid professional was now a possibility in cricket and nearing a possibility in soccer. This is the best thing to happen to both sports – it's created the most wonderful opportunities for female athletes, and also brought about a visible pathway for young girls to aspire to.

Now in Australian cricket, not only are the national squad all full-time, paid professionals, but we are very close to having our entire domestic cohort of female cricketers also being full time. When I started out, just over a decade ago, there weren't even contracts for players and, prior to that, players had to pay their own way on tours.

The most challenging of times when I was playing both sports always revolved around making a decision about which sport to play when there was a clash. Sometimes, those decisions were fairly straightforward, while sometimes they were painstakingly hard. That might sound incredibly selfish, like I was easily picking and choosing which sport I'd show up for on any given day. At times, it may have felt like that to teammates. But those decisions always caused me a lot of angst, mainly because I knew that I would be letting someone down no matter what I decided.

IT CHALLENGED ME PERSONALLY THAT THESE DECISIONS WERE ULTIMATELY ALWAYS MINE TO MAKE – NO ONE ELSE COULD MAKE THEM FOR ME.

I would dread having to call a coach or speak to them at training to let them know that I wouldn't be available for a match or tour. I'd put it off for hours, days if I could, just so as not to have the uncomfortable discussion. I'd lose sleep at the thought of it, be distracted from anything else I was doing or people I was spending time with, and then after I'd made a decision I'd agonise for days over whether I had made the right one and what the fallout would be – what would people think of me? Would they stop putting up with the situation?

But I also knew at the time that this is what I wanted to be doing, this was my dream and the opportunity I was chasing. The uncomfortableness and the anxiety were a small price to pay for what has been one of the highlights of my career, representing my country in two sports that I love.

I'm really glad I stuck at it for as long as I did. I'm also really glad I stopped playing both when I did and just kept going with cricket.

RESILIENCE

I have been asked quite a lot now about how I made the decision to stop playing soccer, and what that felt like. If I'm being honest, the answer I give never really seems to satisfy people who ask. I think they are looking for a pivotal moment, a point in time or a crossroads, where someone forced me to choose, or everything just became too much and I couldn't deal with it. In my mind, this was never the case.

To me, it felt like everything ran its natural course in terms of playing cricket and soccer together.

It was more like one season I was playing both, and when the next one rolled around and so much had happened in the space of eight months, between the end of one W-League and the start of the next one, that I just didn't come back. There was no official announcement, no big meeting; I just spoke to the soccer coach on the phone and we mutually agreed that my continuing to play soccer was going to be too much this time around given the impending cricket schedule.

I never had to say I pick cricket and I'm totally done with soccer. Soccer just slowly petered out. I'm really glad it went this way.

I BELIEVE I OWED IT TO BOTH SPORTS FOR THE CHANGE TO BE TOTALLY UNDRAMATIC, BECAUSE BOTH HAD BEEN SO SUPPORTIVE AND ALWAYS BEEN POSITIVE.

Coming to terms with playing just the one sport seemed to evolve pretty naturally. I just filled up any time that I used to spend training and playing soccer with training and working harder on cricket. This change, the opportunity to spend more time on cricket, certainly helped me mature and develop as a player.

But also, without the soccer experience, and by not specialising in cricket straightaway, I have got more out of myself in the last five years.

The different experiences in soccer, the people I was exposed to, the ways of training and doing things, have all influenced the way I've approached being a professional cricketer. It's helped me have a broader view on things, and a little more acceptance for different methods and thinking.

Most resoundingly, though, I feel like the joy and fun I now have from all the little moments with teammates away from the field has been the best part of playing just the one sport.

KNOWING THAT WE ARE ALL IN IT TOGETHER, AND HAVE EACH OTHER'S BACK, IS PROBABLY THE BEST FORM OF RESILIENCE THERE IS.

When I was playing both soccer and cricket, I certainly missed out on many informal social interactions with people. There were many times when I was leaving straight away after training or matches to get to the next commitment, or missing social events because of schedule clashes.

Those moments are really where all the magic is, where the best stories are created and where friendships for life are forged.

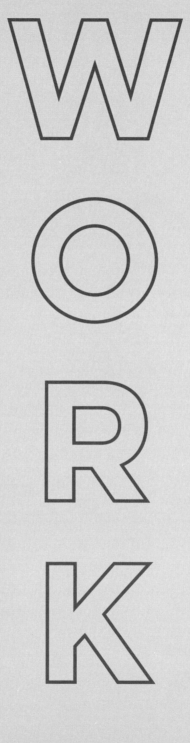

WORK

never thought of working on my cricket as work, but in this analogy, my office was the local nets near home. I wouldn't be able to add up the amount of time I've spent down in those nets. In a lot of ways, all those hours and years are a total blur. Even these days, putting my kitbag in the back of the car and driving down to the nets with Dad in tow is second nature to me when I'm spending any amount of time at home in Sydney.

We first started going down to the local nets when I was five, usually with my brother, Dee. We both took up cricket at the same time. It was probably accidental; I distinctly remember Dad showing Dee how to bowl one evening in the lounge room and asking if he could show me too. The next afternoon we were down at the local nets trying out what Dad had shown us, and by the end of the week we had a 'ball in the sock' rigged up in the backyard for us to practise swinging a bat. I guess, as they say, the rest is history.

It's probably a little funny to say this, but I don't think too much has changed between going down to the nets as a kid and having a session at them now.

AS WE APPROACH THE NETS IN THE CAR, I STILL CROSS MY FINGERS THERE'LL BE A SPARE NET WAITING FOR US.

It was such a deflater if all the nets were full, but if they were, we'd get our bags out of the car and Dad would grab a bat and ball and hit us catches and balls to field until a net became available.

Once we jagged a net, Dad would throw balls and teach us to play as many different shots from the 'textbook' as possible, always making little comments or demonstrating a technical point about the shot. My dad is incredible at this – besides having an amazing eye for technique, he was also a school teacher for many years and has a great way of teaching people. He'd do the same with our bowling, and Dee and I would take turns to bat against each other.

Dee stopped playing cricket not long after he went to high school. I think my dad would attest to this when I say that Dee was a much better cricketer than me. As a little girl, I was in complete awe of how stylish Dee made batting and bowling look. Once Dad showed him the basics of whatever skill, Dee had the pure confidence to repeat it in a smooth and easy manner, without much thought. I've always needed to be way more precise about things, wanting to perfect every single aspect of a skill and happy to spend hours and hours doing that. The way I bat and bowl is far more scripted than Dee's poetic moves with a bat or ball in his hand.

One of the coolest things in recent years is that Dee has started coming back down to the nets with Dad and me, and bowling his leg spin to me. During the week, we'll try and fit a net session in around his lunch break from work, or he'll come down when he's finished for the day.

The three of us back at the local nets has been something I've cherished – with a coffee shout on the line it means it's back to Dee getting me out on a regular basis. But the fact that the three of us are spending time at the nets together again makes me more than happy to take the hit to my ego and shout the coffees!

Without my dad, there's no chance I'd be even remotely capable of playing sport at a decent level. Dad taught me to do everything: throw, catch, kick, pass and hit. And he spent a million and one hours doing it.

In a lot of ways, the special bond that I share with my dad around sport, and in particular cricket, is the reason I play. We've been on this journey together the whole way, from that night when he first showed me how to bowl in the lounge room, to being available at the drop of a hat whenever I want to have a bat or bowl at the nets now. Dad would never want me to feel this way, because he's the most selfless person I know, but any success I have experienced is really our success.

Regardless of where we are in the world, Dad is the last person I speak to before every game of cricket. He still sends me pointers via text message of things to focus on for the match. Dad has this ability to pick up on the smallest things in relation to my game that end up making the biggest difference.

KNOWING I HAVE **SOMEONE WATCHING** SO CLOSELY **WHO KNOWS ME** SO WELL **FILLS ME WITH CONFIDENCE.**

My dad is the most placid person I know. I'm struggling to recall a time when he has ever raised his voice, despite the fact that I would have given him ample opportunity to!

I hate to admit this, but there have been a few times down at the nets when no one else was around that I've thrown a few frustrated words or a tantrum towards him, my bat or anything else in the firing line. Dad always manages to weather those storms with composure. He reminds me of positive things or tells me that he might have thrown a squash racquet once or twice in his time – although I'm not sure I actually believe he did that!

Often those sessions where I get really frustrated for a period end up being our best ones. I know that sounds strange, but once I've managed to get over a hissy fit and realise how much I'm carrying on, it feels like I've broken through a barrier that's been holding me back from getting better at whatever it is I'm working on.

There's something industrious about the word 'work' that I absolutely love. In my opinion, it represents about ninety per cent of what it is to be an elite athlete – working on something, training, preparing to play. The other ten per cent is when the lights come on and you actually play a match, when the goal is to win and entertain people ... Then you're back to working again.

In terms of the sheer time spent, game days are far outweighed by training days. And I love that. I know that probably sounds a little ridiculous, but nothing provides me with a deeper sense of satisfaction and fulfilment than a really hard day of training. The days when you know you pushed yourself, you did everything you could to improve, and whether it pays off in the short term or the long term you know that you got something out of it. If you do that enough times, day in day out, if you keep showing up and working hard, I truly believe it will pay off.

There is so much to learn about yourself from training; likewise, there is so much you can teach yourself by working hard, figuring out what your capable of and where you want to get to next.

TRAINING IS PRACTICALLY A PLAYGROUND TO BE AS INVENTIVE AS YOU LIKE.

Another characteristic that I love about training is that it's not necessarily hard work. Trying a new shot or delivery, tinkering with your batting stance or bowling run-up, doing a new movement in the gym. All of this can be really creative and satisfying. You never know when you might stumble across absolute gold if you keep thinking about different ways of doing things and then try them out.

There are no repercussions if you stuff up in training, only lessons to be learned and things to try.

CONNECTIONS

y junior cricket experience at Oakhill College Cricket Club, where I played until the age of sixteen, is very easy for me to sum up in one word: joyful. I can't think of a single moment where I didn't absolutely love playing junior cricket.

Part of the reason I loved it so much was the time I got to spend with my dad. Most often, he was the one who ferried me around to all the training sessions and matches, always making a servo stop for an ice block on the way home. Besides playing cricket in the backyard or at the local nets, these trips in the car were a big part of the time Dad and I spent together when I was a kid.

When I played in school representative teams, the tournaments would often be somewhere in rural New South Wales. We'd pack up the car, Dad would pick a bunch of his favourite rock cassette tapes to listen to, we'd promise to call Mum once we got to our accommodation, and jump on the road. Gosh, these trips always felt double, if not triple, the length of what they did on the way back, because I'd be riding such a big wave of anticipation to get there and play. During my school years, we did some serious kilometres around New South Wales, staying at a lot of motels and eating dinner at plenty of pubs and RSL clubs.

But the main reason I loved playing junior club cricket as much as I did was my teammates Nathan, Dean and Ben. Some of my fondest memories from this time are of our early Saturday morning matches around Sydney. The four of us would turn up in our whites, dragging our kits behind us, ready to face that week's opponent. Our dads would help us warm up by hitting us catches or throwing balls for us to hit.

Out of the three boys, I met Nathan first, at his dad Simon's 40th birthday party. Simon taught at the same high school as my dad. After we bounced together on the trampoline for about four hours, and Nathan assessed that I could throw a tennis ball at a satisfactory level (which indicated that I could field in the outfield), our friendship was solidified. The next year, I joined the cricket team at Oakhill College, where Simon was the coach and Nathan was the captain, and we have been friends ever since.

I still laugh at how every weekend of the season, after both of us had been dismissed batting, Nath and I would grab a ball and walk around the ground, pegging the ball back and forth while watching the game and sulking. We'd be kicking ourselves at the way in which we got out, and bemoaning the fact that we could have been out there still facing those bowlers if it wasn't for that one shot or one bad decision. In hindsight, that was pretty brattish behaviour and lacked a large amount of sportsmanship, but I guess it was also an early indication of my competitiveness.

One day, Nathan introduced me to this book series called Glory Gardens Cricket Club, which chronicled the fictional trials and tribulations of a local junior cricket team in England. From then on, I was addicted. I'd constantly be dragging Mum into the bookstore to buy the next volume in the series. I loved reading these books, mainly because I always related the team's experiences with our own each weekend. They also had the complete scorecard from each match that was played out in the book, which I'd pore over, looking at the stats for each player in each game and working out the batters' averages and the bowlers' strike rates.

Dean and Ben both joined the team a year or two after me, but once they arrived the four of us became a bit of a gang. We spent lots of time together playing cricket, going to the beach or the movies, and hanging out at each other's houses during school holidays.

Initially, Dean actually played for another team in the same competition and I remember being super-happy when I found out he was coming to play with us at Oakhill College. Dean was the best bowler in the competition and often got me out. He continued to do that at training, but at least then I could keep batting.

Ben's house became kind of the 'spiritual clubhouse' for Oakhill College Cricket Club. Ben's dad comes from a Maltese background and is also a chef. To say that we were well fed would be an understatement.

Although I don't see them as often these days, I'd like to think there will always be a special bond between Nath, Dean, Ben and me. I owe them all a huge amount for teaching me the value of mateship, and what is truly

ALL THOSE **HUMAN SENSATIONS** YOU GET FROM **HAVING GENUINE** FRIENDSHIPS WITH PEOPLE – **NOTHING IS BETTER THAN THAT.**

important when it comes to sport. I don't really remember many of the actual games we played for Oakhill College – the scores and outcomes seem irrelevant now.

But I do remember the moments off the field: Nath and I playing together at the cricket ground long after the match was finished; the long beach days we spent down at Manly during the summer holidays; playing backyard cricket in between swimming in the pool at Ben's house; Dean picking me up in his little green Charade and driving me down to the park to kick a football.

I'll cherish those memories for the rest of my life, and I hope one day when we are old that our kids will have similar experiences – preferably with each other.

s an athlete, there are many advantages to having routines around training, exercise and diet, but there's also a danger: that you'll become one-dimensional and think there's nothing of any importance in the world outside of your next match. I feel it's especially important for athletes to be inquisitive about what's outside their bubble.

When I think of my favourite memories from my sporting career, a huge number of them are in and around the sport, certainly, but they don't always directly involve playing sport.

If I'm on tour, I want there to be more to the tour than just cricket. I don't want to come home having seen hotel rooms, buses and fields, but nothing else. One of the things I enjoy most on tour is being able to talk with people – my teammates, the support staff and, when possible, the people I come across along the way who have a story to tell.

Whenever we get some spare time, particularly in a new country, I also love the opportunity to explore the place we're visiting. Usually, my favourite way to do this is on foot, or by bike, hunting for cool scenery or something unique to that location. You always see a lot more when you're at ground level, going at a slower pace, rather than whizzing past in a car or bus. It's the fun, often spontaneous, special moments I've really wanted to seek out – those moments you can sometimes miss by being solely focused on sport. The random moments you can't cultivate, the ones that just happen – those are the ones that stay with you forever.

These connections make me a better person and a better athlete, too, because when you step into the real world you realise that what you're doing is not the be-all and end-all.

Playing my sport is certainly something to be enjoyed and to be grateful for. But talking with my teammates between matches has much more meaning to me than a lot of the things we do on the field. I truly appreciate their company and the moments we've shared together.

I WANT TO **SEE MY TEAMMATES AS MORE THAN WORK COLLEAGUES** I HAVE TO DO A JOB WITH. I WANT TO **HAVE FRIENDSHIPS WITH THEM THAT LAST** A LOT **LONGER THAN OUR CAREERS** WILL.

B A L A
N C E.

BALANCE

alance is having a conscious understanding and awareness of the world around you. In today's society, where we are so often engaged with things like social media and communication, maintaining a balance can be challenging for so many of us. There is so much opportunity to access information about yourself, a lot of it unhelpful or distracting. At the end of the day we are just playing a game and it's not for sheep stations and it's not life and death. It's not that important. Maintaining a balance and keeping things in perspective is invaluable.

One thing my mum always said to me, going back to when I was a nervous wreck before athletics carnivals and swimming carnivals and cross-country carnivals and me not wanting to go, was:

'THE WORST THING YOU CAN DO IS NOT TURN UP. BECAUSE YOU'LL KNOW YOU DIDN'T EVEN TRY TO HAVE A GO. YOU'LL NEVER KNOW WHAT MIGHT HAVE HAPPENED.'

I've always remembered that, the benefit of just putting yourself on a starting line and seeing what might happen from there. The other thing I learned was that when I left at the end, no one else was waking up or going to bed thinking about whether I had won a race or not. It could be part of my day. It could be a great personal challenge and a step out of my comfort zone. I could run away from being under pressure but, by nightfall, I'd be feeling flat. Who won? What happened?

You can think everyone's watching you and judging you and talking about you when really, they're not. They have their own lives to be interested in.

In the grand scheme of things, it's not that big a deal. I'm just not that important.

It. Just. Does. Not. Matter.

have to remind myself of that still because, of course, in its own way, what we do with our lives is going to matter. It should matter. It's meaningful because it does matter. But it's not the only thing that matters.

There's no distinguishing feature that separates professional athletes from anybody else. We're all normal people. There's nothing that different between us and people who have office jobs.

Still, it seems drilled into athletes, in our relatively closed environments, that you are special. People are far more willing to open doors for you and offer you things you don't necessarily need or could easily pay for yourself. It is so contradictory that the more you already have can make some people keen to try to give you even more, or to want to be associated with you in some way or another.

It ties in, massively, with the problems of entitlement and an inflated sense of importance. In an athlete's world, you roll your ankle and it becomes the biggest issue in the world. In the scheme of life, it's not a huge deal, it will heal pretty quickly. But everything gets catastrophised in elite sport because we think what is going on with us is more important than real-life issues.

My family and friends – they're who I want to prosper. Which is the case for most people, but because being an athlete is such a selfish vocation, it's easy to forget there's a lot of other issues outside the sporting environment that are far more important.

If I'm going to be admired, I want to be admired for how I've done something, not what I've done. How I've done it as a person.

he grand scheme of things – I like that term. I think it has the power to pull you out of your own self-centred world, or the immediate situation that feels all-encompassing. Keeping in mind the grand scheme of things helps you maintain a much broader sense of what is really going on. It gives you the ability to deal much better with the little things that have the capacity to cause more anxiousness and stress than they should. Losing a game that you should have won, injuring yourself and missing a game, or not being able to do something in a training session you really wanted to are, at worst, minor hiccups or bumps along the road, and at best great learning opportunities. But you can only see them as those things if you keep in mind the much bigger picture of who you are and what you are doing.

But our place in the world can seem out of whack. People are too willing to make excuses for you. If you miss a family member's birthday everyone says, 'Oh that's okay, she's so busy'. I don't want it to be like that. Everyone's busy. We all have commitments and places we have to be and things we have to manage. I guess it's easy for people to put athletes on a pedestal, and then it becomes easy for athletes to think they deserve to be on a pedestal. Every time we're on tour I think, 'Wow, we're getting treated pretty well here'. Beautiful hotels. Nice meals. We get to travel to some amazing parts of the world, with friends, to play a game. There's no way I'm complaining about it. I think the main thing is to appreciate it and not take it for granted. To not think this is the way real life is. I don't want to come home from a trip and think, 'Well, where's my room service dinner?' I want to see it for what it is. Something to be incredibly grateful about, for as long as it lasts, which is not going to be forever. I don't think being good at something should define who you are.

If I'm walking down the street thinking I play for Australia at sport, that's going to influence everything I do as a person. I don't think it should be a defining part of an athlete's make-up.

Sometimes things go your way and that's really great. Sometimes they don't go your way. They go someone else's way. It can all change very quickly.

Some of it is going to be out of your control. You simply can't win everything.

That's what Michael Jordan is getting at when he says it hasn't been a non-stop highlights reel for him, either. Jordan was famous for his buzzer-beating shots, the shots that won the game in the last moment. But if Jordan made every one of his shots, where would the thrill be in making any one of them?

My favourite quote of his is about failure as much as success. The failures that sit alongside all the successes. The failures that lead to the successes.

I VALUE BEING ABLE TO TAKE A DEEP BREATH AND SEE WHERE EACH DAY AND GAME AND TRAINING SESSION SITS IN THE BIGGER PICTURE.

In the context of life.
In the grand scheme of things.

here is such an aversion in sport and society to becoming unbalanced, or overly consumed in your vocation that your entire life starts revolving around what it is that you do. I totally understand this phobia and the willingness to live a well-rounded life. I've said that it doesn't have to be the be-all and end-all. But with the things you are doing, I think you may as well go all-in with them.

Balance is important for health and wellbeing, but purpose is, too. There's a clear difference between doing something as well as you possibly can, by putting in huge amounts of effort day in and day out, and letting what you're doing define you as a person so that everything hinges on being successful in your chosen field. I think that's what I'm trying to say. I get passionate about the craft, but I don't want the whole experience to hinge on the results. You may not exactly achieve life balance in your pursuit to be one of the best in what it is that you do, but you can still maintain an identity, a perspective and a connection to things that are important to you in the broader scheme of life.

I genuinely believe that to be successful in any competitive industry, you have to put in more time and effort than almost anyone else. But that doesn't mean you have to let your chosen pursuit become the essence of who you are.

In fact, I think it's when this happens that you don't necessarily achieve what it is you want to anyway. You lose sight of why you started doing it in the first place. And you attach far too much value to the outcome and how that reflects on you as a person, rather than appreciating and enjoying the process of getting there.

To be so passionate about something, and so motivated to do well, that you are willing to get to work/training before anyone else, leave after everyone else, or come in on a day that everyone else has off, is in my mind a blessing and a great mindset to have. Similarly, doing things with a greater intensity or enthusiasm can often have the same results and require no more time. I think this is something worth celebrating and embracing, rather than shirking away from it or letting others talk you out of spending extra time working on things, especially if they're saying that to make themselves feel better about not doing extra.

I'm certainly not saying that this should become all you do. Maintaining relationships and devoting time to family and close friends is vital. So too is doing other things that you enjoy and that make you and the people you care for happy. Maybe that's where the whole balance thing comes into it? It's amazing how many hours in a day you have available when you prioritise and plan what you want to get done and you're efficient and energetic with the way you do it. Those who are closest to you, the ones who truly care for you, will have an innate understanding of what you're trying to achieve and will want to do everything they can to help you along the way. They'll share the ups and downs and take great pleasure in being a part of your journey.

I'm pinching too many Michael Jordan quotes, but here are two more that resonate with me:

'I can accept failure; everyone fails at something. But I can't accept not trying.'

'You must expect great things of yourself before you can do them.'

– MICHAEL JORDAN

Of course, the risk with all of this is that you do absolutely everything you can, and put in all the effort you can muster, and things don't work out or you don't achieve what you want to. That can be gut-wrenching, a true lesson in resilience and a reminder of how important the support of others can be.

However, in my opinion, the even greater risk is to never take the chance, to never dive fully in and to then spend the rest of your life asking, 'What if?'

I LOVE TRAINING.
IT'S PROBABLY
MY FAVOURITE
PART OF BEING
AN ATHLETE.

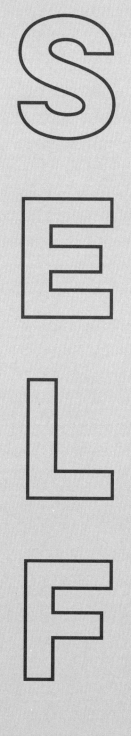

SELF

t would be remiss of me not to mention my mum, Kathy, when talking about being down at the nets. Alongside my dad, my mum is my other hero. Neither have ever been pushy parents towards Dee or me, and they have always been determined to provide us both with the support and opportunities to do anything we were passionate about.

For example, Mum has one day off a week from work, on a Thursday. If I'm having a hit with Dad on Thursday, Mum always comes down with our dog, who chases after balls that have gone astray. It makes me feel bad that Mum does this on her only day off, but she refuses to not help out, saying that way we can hit more balls because it's saving us time not having to go and pick them up.

THOSE NETS ARE AMONG MY FAVOURITE PLACES ON EARTH BECAUSE THEY ARE WHERE I FEEL MOST LIKE MYSELF.

In so many ways, our local nets represent my family and my childhood. There are so many memories and moments wrapped up down there. I value the fact that I've been able to hold onto this connection to my childhood and my mum, my dad and my brother. Without being too whimsical about it, the link to my family makes cricket seem simple to me. It takes away a lot of the fuss that doesn't really matter.

It's the same principle that my dad taught me when I was younger: work on something until you are able to perfect it and put it in your toolbox.

What makes it worthwhile is doing it with people who you care a lot about and who you want to share those experiences, moments and memories with.

Quite a lot has changed in my life and around me, but since I was five I've been setting foot in those synthetic grass cages and going through the same processes with the same people I love.

There's this turn of phrase that often gets used in athlete parlance, which I am totally guilty of saying on numerous occasions, but it's also quite off the mark in terms of reality. That phrase is in reference to 'normal people', as if being an elite athlete sets you outside the bounds of being a normal person.

'That's what normal people would do.'

'For normal people this wouldn't be the case.'

The irony is that no one could ever define what being a 'normal person' is because life is so varied and nuanced.

I don't like using this phrase, because it assumes that being good at a sport sets you apart on the scale of normality. It leads to this mindset that elite athletes are special and that what we do should be considered in a different light to other jobs. In the worst case, it can provide a 'get out of jail free' card for shirking responsibility and can create a sense of entitlement.

couldn't write a book without having a small section on coffee. Coffee is a big part of my life and representative of a number of things. I'm actually someone who doesn't have much of a response to caffeine, so you could argue that I'm wasting my time with it. But my love for coffee goes far beyond the hit of energy it provides. The social act of sitting down to have a coffee is something I love to do with people of all walks of life, whether they be friends, colleagues or people I'm meeting for the first time.

I love the fact that when you put a cup of coffee between two people it provides a platform for them to converse about all kinds of things and tends to take away any potential awkwardness. Now that I think of it, some of the best conversations I've had with people have been over a coffee.

When I'm on tour or find myself away from home for some reason, one of the first things I do is look for a local spot that is into their coffee. Then I'll chuck on a pair of runners and make my way there. I like being able to sit among locals who all have their own coffee routines. It gives me a sense for the city I'm in, knowing that I have at least one thing in common with everyone else in the cafe. I actually keep a record of the coffee shops I've been to – I want to remember in case I return to a city.

More often than not, one thing in common turns into two if the owner is around, because in most situations, no matter where I am in the world, if there's a good coffee spot about, there's an Australian behind the counter.

I'm really happy to head to a local coffee shop by myself, but often on tour there's a strong contingent of players and staff who are also on the hunt for a decent cup. It's common to see a bunch of us leaving the hotel in our downtime to go and sit in a cafe for a while.

P E R

S E V

E R A

N C E

PERSEVERANCE

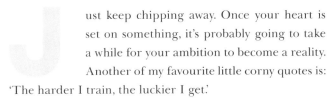

Just keep chipping away. Once your heart is set on something, it's probably going to take a while for your ambition to become a reality. Another of my favourite little corny quotes is: 'The harder I train, the luckier I get.'

You try hard. It doesn't come off. You try hard. It doesn't come off. You try hard. It doesn't come off. You try hard. It comes off! Because of perseverance.

IT MIGHT TAKE **A HUNDRED TRAINING SESSIONS TO MASTER SOMETHING,** BUT FOR ME, **THERE'S A LOT OF JOY IN THE PROCESS ITSELF.**

It might not be what you'd normally call fun, but I do think there's some deep and proper joy in it. If you're really determined to get better at something, at the very least, if you do the work, you're not going to be any worse at it. Any improvement is worth it.

---

have thrown a number of cricket bats across a number of nets in my time because it's been so frustrating and, in that moment, felt hopeless.

There are still lots of things I can't nail from a batting perspective, with two aspects I've focused on for the last few years. First, consistently hitting the ball over cover. Second, consistently hitting a sweep. Neither of them is a natural shot for me, but I'm a million times better at them now than I was a year and a half ago. After all that time of trying to get good at those shots, I'm still not happy with them.

I spend so many hours on them, and I love that.

One of the processes I enjoy at training is to improve something I'm not that good at. Experimenting with different techniques. Coming up with different drills to try.

You chip away, chip away. Your strengths are always going to be your strengths. They're the easy things to practise and they're good for your confidence and they can give you a sense of security, knowing there's something you're good at.

Quite often, though, I get more of a buzz working on the things I'm not so good at. In the back of my mind, I know the more balls I hit and the more I practice and try to perfect it, when I get into a game situation and try to hit a sweep, the more likely I am to make contact with the middle of the ball, rather than the ball hitting me on the head or somewhere else on my body.

THE NATURAL INSTINCT TAKES OVER, AND THE MUSCLE MEMORY YOU'VE INGRAINED IN YOURSELF, AND YOU START DOING IT WITHOUT THINKING TWICE.

I'm not a confident sweeper and I'm so terrible at it in the nets, but there have been times in games when I've played it on instinct and thought, 'My God, it worked! Act cool. Don't let anyone know you have no idea what you're doing!'

I know for a fact that if I hadn't played sweep shots multiple times in the nets, and by multiple I mean thousands of times, I would never have been able to do it in a match. My body would not have gone there. It would not have known the movements. I knew I had to learn it. You just do it and do it and do it until it becomes more comfortable.

You do it until you start to get that nice, small glimmer of confidence. And then all the net sessions and bat-throwings are worth it.

he shots you've persevered with are the ones you end up remembering. You could have gone with a game plan in your career to just never play that shot. The sweep is something you don't have to do. You end up not remembering too many cover drives when you've always been able to play them. You haven't really proved anything new to yourself. You know you can do that.

Sometimes, I think about how cool it is that we can create quite a strong sense of connection with people when we observe one another persevering with something. Particularly in a sporting team, where you're presented fairly regularly with challenges, both as a collective and individually, perseverance is so important in terms of keeping people motivated and on the right track. My sweep shot analogy is a relatively unimportant analogy about perseverance, but the fact is that a lot of the team know it's something I struggle with, and so when I manage to play one in a game they are genuinely stoked for me.

In a similar vein, observing a teammate coming back from a significant injury and dealing with all the challenges of trying to get their body to do what it used to do again is impressive. The isolation that injury sometimes creates could be enough to make a person want to throw in the towel on any given day and just get out of there. But there's always something that keeps them going, doing mundane, repetitive exercises and trying to teach themselves to move again in the way that they took for granted before they got injured. I believe that a large part of that something is perseverance and, ultimately, perseverance is the thing that gives you a very special sense of fulfilment when things come right.

WHEN YOU'RE PRESENTED FAIRLY REGULARLY **WITH CHALLENGES,** BOTH AS A COLLECTIVE AND INDIVIDUALLY, **PERSEVERANCE IS SO IMPORTANT** IN TERMS OF **KEEPING PEOPLE MOTIVATED** AND **ON THE RIGHT TRACK.**

PERSEVERANCE IS WHAT GIVES YOU A VERY SPECIAL SENSE OF FULFILMENT WHEN THINGS COME RIGHT.

OPPORTUNITY

n many ways, the word 'opportunity' carries with it quite a lot of privilege. Growing up in the country I have, in the home I did, in the area where we lived, with the parents and family I have, I'm well aware that this has provided me with access to opportunities that a lot of other people have never been afforded. So in writing about the notion of opportunities and making the most of them, I know I've had many more than most. It has given me a significant head start, and got me to the starting line much quicker, and without much struggle.

The abundance of opportunity someone is exposed to is definitely an advantage, but I'm not certain that it's the amount you are afforded that really matters. It's more about capitalising on the opportunity that does come your way, even if it's one you're not totally sure about or hesitant to take because you're anxious about whether it will work out, if you'll be any good at it or if you'll enjoy it. But, if that's the worst case – if you don't enjoy it or it doesn't go to plan – then, at the very least, you'll still gain a new experience from doing it. And, quite probably, you'll learn something about yourself at the same time.

It might not end up being the opportunity you had planned on getting either, and often that can be disheartening. But to reflect on a popular saying, 'When one door closes, another door opens,' I believe that if you keep opening doors when they come along, there's no way you won't be a better person for it. Most likely, you'll get to where you want to go, even if it's not by the most direct path.

OPPORTUNITIES COME AT DIFFERENT TIMES AND THEY CAN COME OUT OF NOWHERE, BUT THE TRICK IS TO BE PREPARED TO POUNCE AS SOON AS THEY DO.

y first opportunity as a cricketer was being picked for a junior boys' team. Sydney junior cricket has representative competitions through all the age groups from Under-11s, including the Creak Shield and the Cawsey Shield.

As a kid, I remember the biggest bonus about being picked in these teams is that you got to play on a Sunday as well as your normal Saturday games, so your whole weekend revolved around cricket. Dad might have been rolling his eyes about having to do more driving, but he actually loved it. So did I.

Every game was a chance to get picked for the next game, or the next year in the next age group. Competing with the best boy players, I really loved that. I wanted to try out for everything, play against everyone, in school teams, in any teams that would have me.

riginally, I considered calling this chapter 'Debut' and writing more about the first time I played professionally, but the more I thought about it I realised I view those initial games as opportunities and as starting points. To me, a debut is very much just one moment in time, a one-off experience that doesn't last long.

I don't remember much about the first game I played for Australia, in either cricket or soccer – how the team played, how I played, the exact score or anything particularly specific about the matches themselves. They are all vague recollections. I'm not in any way meaning to diminish what those two games meant to me: they were very special occasions, and moments that I will cherish because I was so lucky to share them with some amazing people.

The reason they've become so vague in my mind is because I wasn't content with them. I think I realised quite quickly, perhaps even before those games started, that I wanted to keep playing sport for as long as I possibly could and that a one-off game, as exciting as it was doing it for the first time, wasn't going to satisfy me. That probably sounds slightly contradictory, I know.

EVEN THOUGH I WASN'T CONTENT, WHAT I REMEMBER WAS AN OVERWHELMING SENSE OF FULFILMENT, OF FEELING LIKE I'D FOUND EXACTLY WHAT I'D LOVE TO CONTINUE DOING.

Those initial experiences on tour with the team, travelling, training and playing my first matches, gave me a deep-seated motivation and desire to make the most of it every time I get the opportunity.

Around the time of my debuts, whether it was conscious or not, I made a pretty strong commitment to myself that I was going to try to be in this for the long haul, or at least for as long as I feel the same sense of joy and fulfilment from playing that I do at the moment.

When my first tour to Darwin with the Australian Cricket Team finished, I remember being bitterly disappointed. The day I returned home, I was moping around the house, missing the company of the other girls in the team and the excitement of being busy all day. Mum and Dad simply laughed at me when I self-diagnosed a case of 'post-tour blues' – and then they said that was absolutely no excuse not to go to school the next day.

———

o many of the things I've experienced still feel surreal and unexplainable. Nothing more so than when I was initially selected for the Australian Women's Cricket Team. If I'm ever asked to recount this story, I genuinely feel like I'm making it up. I was in Year 11 at school when I found out I had been selected for a series against New Zealand to be played in Darwin in July 2007.

There were many incredible aspects about my selection, but probably nothing more surprising than the fact that I hadn't yet played senior-level domestic cricket. I'd only played underage representative cricket for New South Wales and been on just one tour with the Under-21 Australian team to New Zealand. My selection was pretty out there – I was very much an unproven player and it blew my socks off – so I can't imagine what other people thought about it at the time.

During morning tea one day, Dad called Jess, my best mate at school, who had a mobile phone, to let me know that the Head Selector at the time, Marg Jennings, had called our home phone to say I had been selected. When Jess passed me her phone (a Motorola Razr flip-phone in bright pink) and said it's your dad, I remember not really believing what Dad was saying. I didn't even know there was a series happening that July. I hung up from talking to him, handed back the phone to Jess, told her what had happened, made her promise not to tell anyone and then flatly refused to believe it was true for the rest of the day.

It wasn't until I got home from school and Dad had me call Marg back, when she told me I should head to training at the Sydney Cricket Ground the next evening to meet the other NSW-based girls that it started to finally sink in what was happening.

THE BEST OPPORTUNITIES CAN BE THE SMALL ONES. IF YOU MAKE THE MOST OF ENOUGH SMALL OPPORTUNITIES, THEY BUILD INTO SOMETHING BIG.

hen I got to play that first game in Darwin, I told myself I could only do what I could do. I was definitely nervous. When the selector knocked on the door and told me I would actually be playing, I didn't know what to do. When something major happens and you're far from home, how are you meant to react? I couldn't just sit there and watch TV.

So I put on my joggers and took off to a park down the road. I didn't really know what to do when I got to the park, so I pretended to bowl. Without a ball. I did my proper run-up and did my proper delivery in this park, all on my own, which must have looked ridiculous to anyone who saw it. It felt ridiculous to the person doing it!

I bowled these invisible balls for five to ten minutes because I was thinking, 'Oh my, I'm playing tomorrow, do some work to get ready. Do some drills. Do something!' Nobody else in the team knew I was doing it. Thankfully. That probably would have earned me a bit of teasing. I shadow-bowled in that random Darwin park one day and then the next day I was bowling for Australia. The whole thing still feels as bizarre as it did the day Dad got the phone call, and the day I got the knock on the door.

imilarly, with soccer, getting selected felt bizarre and slightly fanciful. I was still on my first cricket tour in Darwin that July when I received an email about a young team heading over to Hong Kong to fill in for the Matildas during an Olympic qualifying match. Essentially, the Young Matildas would play instead of the senior team, so that they didn't have to travel, as the qualifying match was a bit null and void. Officially, though, it meant that anyone who played in the match would be capped as a full senior international player.

When we went to Hong Kong to play, I remember thinking this is a cool starting point, and that I'd love to improve enough to have the opportunity to earn a cap playing with the full senior side at some point.

Call it naivety, or maybe it was more intentional than that, but at no stage did I think of that period over a few weeks in Year 11, when I played both cricket and soccer for Australia, as a particularly big deal. I genuinely had no awareness of what other people thought of it, nor much interest in what they thought, to be honest. Also, I didn't think much about what it might mean for me in the future. I just knew I want to keep doing this. And how do I keep doing this?

I think this was the point when my belief began that to constantly be aware of, or on the lookout for, opportunities, no matter how big or small, is the one way of ensuring you make the most of things. It probably sounds obvious and simple, but I remember the number of times I've been hesitant to do something or thought about saying no. Often, why I've hesitated has been for silly reasons too, like when I've been self-conscious or shy, or was a bit tired at the time.

If it hadn't been for me stopping for a second to think about the reason I was saying no, and what the worst case scenario would be if it didn't go well, there would be a number of things I would have missed out on which have ended up having a big impact on me in a positive way.

I always come back to this, and I apologise for being boring, that at the most fundamental level of being an athlete something as simple as always turning up to training, and viewing it each time as an opportunity to be better, to learn something new or, at the very least, to have fun, can make a significant difference to a day you're lacking purpose or a bit of motivation.

I am naturally pretty shy, especially around new people, and I practically have a phobia about having phone calls with strangers. Being on my own in a social situation with people I don't know is probably the most uncomfortable situation I can imagine. My immediate reaction to anything that involves meeting new people or being in a public setting on my own is to run away or avoid it at all costs. But there have also been a lot of new people who I've been initially so nervous to meet that I've almost backed out, or when I've met them I've come across fairly guarded and probably made them second guess me.

There are two people I think of straightaway who have had a profound effect on me, both from a sport perspective and far more generally in terms of my life: Ben Sawyer, our Sydney Sixers Head Coach and Australian Assistant Coach, and Ben Serpell, the Head Strength and Conditioning Coach at the Brumbies rugby team in Canberra. In both instances, I almost ran away from the opportunity to work with the Bens because I was too anxious and self-conscious. With a fair bit of encouragement, I managed to get over my uncomfortableness during our initial interactions and, as a result, have been fortunate enough to have the most incredible opportunity of working with them for the last seven or so years.

I want to mention both these guys, firstly, because they have become friends for life and, secondly, because I think they are representative in my life of the incredible power people can have in terms of broadening your opportunities. They have made me aware of things in relation to sport I had never even contemplated before. Both are incredible confidants who are always there to listen but, equally, they always have a solution or means of helping me improve when I'm a bit stuck.

I feel indebted to them because they have made me believe I am capable of far more than I ever thought possible and have shown me how to do it. The opportunity I've had to work with them is something I will feel forever grateful for, and also something I will never be able to truly repay.

> WHATEVER IT IS, **UNLESS YOU HAVE AN INCREDIBLY GOOD REASON** TO DO SO, **DON'T CLOSE THE DOOR** ON AN OPPORTUNITY **TOO QUICKLY.**

The notion of recognising an opportunity and making the most of it is so varied – sometimes, you may not even know it's an opportunity until you're in the thick of it. I believe you could classify an opportunity as, essentially, just being anything that is new – a new experience, a new person to work with, a new way of doing things, a new team, a new location.

My high school has a saying that often pops into mind these days – 'a world of opportunity'. That's what I have been so unfathomably lucky to have.

I WANT TO **MAKE THE MOST OF EVERY SINGLE OPPORTUNITY** RELATED TO PLAYING SPORT, **ON THE FIELD AND OFF THE FIELD,** BECAUSE I'VE BEEN SO **UNBELIEVABLY LUCKY TO GET A CHANCE** IN THE FIRST PLACE.

I DON'T WANT TO LOOK BACK AND WISH I HAD TRIED HARDER.

DET
ERMI
NAT
ION

DETERMINATION

**W**hen I write notes before a match, 'determination' is one of the words I put at the bottom of the page each time. I like the strength the word implies, the single-mindedness that you sometimes require to do what you want to do. It reminds me of that odd occasion when you look into someone's eyes and see a steely reserve, as though they have complete and utter clarity about what they're going to do and how they're going to do it. There's no obstacle or impediment that is going to deter them, they're just going to give it everything they've got.

SIMPLY BEING DETERMINED CAN GET YOU A LONG WAY TOWARDS WHERE YOU WANT TO GO.

I often think people with real determination are the most imposing competitors on the sporting field. They are the ones who keep bouncing back from any hit you land on them and do not stop fighting until the match is over. A team full of determined players is an even more scary proposition, because you know, no matter how your team lines up with them on paper, they're never going to be easybeats.

IF IT'S WORTH DOING,
IT'S WORTH OVERDOING.

love this phrase. It's a motivating way of saying that if you're going to do something you may as well go all-in and do it to the absolute best of your ability. Get caught up in it. Turn it into an experience that you can take a lot away from. To me, there are two parts to maximising the time you spend doing something. The first part is purely putting in effort. The second is developing clear processes and routines that provide direction towards what you want to achieve. Doing these things consistently enables you to immerse yourself in whatever it is you're doing. They also stop me getting too caught up or overwhelmed by what I'm doing. I've found that if I have a clear purpose, and a mapped-out way of how I'm going to go about it, then I know where to start, what I should be able to achieve on any given day, and when I can walk away from it satisfied for the time being.

Everyone's routines and processes are particular to them. That's one of the great things about sport – there are many ways to skin a cat – but, essentially, all routines and processes serve the same purpose: they provide focus, a sense of control and a means of getting to where you want to go. From my experiences, how much people need to rely on them depends on their personality. There are girls like me in our team who are meticulous and unwavering about doing what works for them, and others who go with the flow, relax and let things happen more naturally.

The one negative thing about being determined and immersing yourself in something is that it has the potential to give you a bit of tunnel vision, especially when you're still trying to figure things out. There have been times when I've been so driven or determined to do something that I've missed what's going on around me or had a complete lack of awareness of other people.

Notably, when I was younger, there were many times when I'd be so focused on what I wanted to do at training that I'd almost not realise there were other people around.

There's a story that Elyse Villani, one of my teammates, tells that I'm not one bit proud of, but we laugh about it now. I must have been twenty-one or twenty-two at the time and we were on tour in Sydney. Whenever we tour in Australia, we have those big eight-seater hire vans to ferry everyone around. We were arriving at a recovery session down at Bondi Beach, and I was so wrapped up in my own thoughts about what I wanted to do at recovery – how long I'd spend in the water, what stretches I'd do and so on – that I hopped out of the van thinking I was the last person, shut the door right in Elyse's face and walked off! I had no awareness she was behind me, and one of the other girls had to go back and open the door for her. I just walked off, probably already starting a hamstring stretch.

———

Finding a balance is important, between being determined and doing everything you can to achieve what you want while also being patient and taking in what's in front of you, knowing that not everything goes perfectly to plan. Learning to adapt when your plans are not going perfectly makes you far more resilient, and more enjoyable to be around!

TO ME, **DETERMINATION** IS ESSENTIALLY **BEING ABLE TO COMPROMISE** ON THINGS, **WITHOUT ACTUALLY COMPROMISING** ON ANYTHING.

There are always ways to do the things you want to, even when other responsibilities or situations get in the way, as they often do. Perhaps what eventuates isn't the way you had it planned out in your head, but it doesn't make it any less valuable or worthwhile.

A clear example of this for me is that I really, really value doing simple batting and bowling drills at training sessions on tour.

THEY ARE **FUNDAMENTAL TO HOW I PREPARE,** BECAUSE THEY **GIVE ME A LOT OF CONFIDENCE** THAT THE **FOUNDATIONS OF MY GAME ARE GOING WELL.**

In my mind, when under pressure in games, if I've made sure I'm doing all the basic skills right, those simple things will be second nature for me to execute when I'm under the pump.

Sometimes we run out of time at training to fit these in – there's time pressure to let another team on the turf wickets or the bus is leaving to take everyone back to the hotel. In these cases, and I'm certainly not the only one to do this, I either use the grass outfield rather than the turf wickets to do my drills, or come back later in the day in a taxi with a poor coach who I've harassed into throwing some balls to me outside of the session. If we've been training in Sydney, I've caught a cab home to our local nets and met Dad to do the drills. None of those scenarios is ideal, or how I'd plan to do things if I could help it, but I'm determined to do those drills because I know they're super important to how I perform. And while it's very important not to negatively impact the team, it's also my responsibility to the team to be prepared to the best of my ability. There is always a way to compromise without compromising.

This might sound a bit odd to a lot of people, but sometimes I think that the matches we play are actually the least enjoyable part of being an athlete. Training sessions are when you experiment and tinker and see the areas you can push yourself. They aren't so much about officially winning or losing, they're more about learning and gaining. In the nets, I can hit a thousand balls if I want to. I can concentrate on feel and routines and the little details I love, there are no time restraints. It's when you can be honest with yourself and admit your weaknesses and express yourself.

In a match, there's pressure to perform, there are restrictions on you in terms of the game situation and what you need to do to help the team win. I might walk out to bat and face one ball and that's it, I could bowl one over and be whacked around the park, I could drop a crucial catch or misfield and see the ball go for four. One mistake or piece of bad luck and you're out.

PLAY ONE BAD SHOT AS A BATTER AND YOU MIGHT BE OUT. PROPERLY OUT. OUT OF THE GAME.

You can be in great form but you get a bit unlucky and you're on your way. It can take a millisecond. You get used to it, but it's a tightrope walk.

Of course, those are all dire straits, worst-case scenario examples, and when matches go well there's always a lot of joy in knowing that we were successful.

Not many sports have such a small margin for error. If you hit a bad golf shot, you don't have to walk back to the clubhouse. If you serve a fault in tennis, you get another serve!

TRAINING SESSIONS ARE WHEN YOU EXPERIMENT AND TINKER AND SEE THE AREAS YOU CAN PUSH YOURSELF.

hen I'm playing a match, rather peculiarly I guess, I usually stand up the whole time I'm waiting to bat. I stand up in the dressing room until it's my turn to go out there. I might sit down between overs or during a drinks break, but the majority of the time I'm on my feet.

In the dressing room, all you can do is think. There's literally nothing else to do. You might feel like hitting a few balls as a warm-up, but you can't. If you have to bat, you don't want to go running out to the pitch.

When you're waiting to bat, you're there with all your teammates. That's comforting. You have allies, some encouraging words, your friends. But then you have to say goodbye to them and head off to see what you can do for them.

It's a surreal moment when you first start walking out. Not quite as bad as being on your own in a school athletics carnival, but for however many seconds it takes to get out there, it's close. There's a bit of shock. You're actually in. You're walking into the middle of a picture you've been looking at. You're walking out as if you're on auto-pilot, but by the time you get to the pitch, it feels very real.

When you walk out to the pitch, irrespective of what you've been doing while waiting, everything snaps into focus. Now I'm thinking about nothing but batting and what I have to do. What I want to do. How I want to play.

You go from the position of spectator, knowing that at some point you'll be out there. But it's up in the air, you don't know what's going to happen and when, all that uncertainty! Then it's your turn and you're actually walking out. It's happening. It's happening right now. You're trying to remember all the things you've told yourself to remember.

It's the loneliest time in cricket.

WALKING OUT TO THE PITCH, FROM THE DRESSING ROOM OR THE DUGOUT, YOU'RE ENTIRELY ON YOUR OWN.

n cricket, Test matches are probably the greatest determinant and examination of character that exists in the game. The sheer duration of a match can make it arduous, asking you to keep turning up and putting in effort when you've probably had enough for the time being. Women play four-day Tests, instead of five-day Tests like the men, so there's more need to maintain a decent run rate. Tests are also unforgiving in terms of needing to focus.

YOU NEVER KNOW WHEN A PIVOTAL MOMENT IS GOING TO COME ALONG THAT MIGHT HAVE A HUGE IMPACT ON THE COURSE OF A MATCH.

If you're not ready for it, then it can be so costly. Physically they're a challenge – there is so much repetition and the need to constantly perform a skill well over many hours. In my opinion, these same factors also make Test cricket the most enjoyable and satisfying format of the game.

During Test matches, you're out there all day, they're physically and mentally demanding, and then you get to wake up the next day and do it again. And again. And again. You put everything into a day, but you go home that night still in the middle of a battle. The game's still on.

It brings up all sorts of situations that you want to capitalise on or reverse. Stumps is a chance for everyone to get away, gauge exactly where everything stands and then make their next move the following day.

We don't play a lot of Tests in women's cricket, usually just one every couple of years against England in an Ashes series, so they're pretty rare and incredibly special to be a part of. When one comes around, everyone is excited about the opportunity.

We normally have quite a few debutants in each game, which is really cool, too. It makes the first morning of the game special, as the debutants are presented with their

baggy green in front of the team and all their family and friends who have come to support them.

I've played in about eight Tests in the last twelve years, so I still feel like a complete novice at the format, but I do absolutely love and relish the opportunity to play Test cricket. They've certainly been some of the biggest highlights of my career, especially the ones when we've managed to win the match. Of the eight I have played in, I've been part of two victories, two losses and four draws. The two wins were some of the most satisfying games of cricket I've ever played.

The first Test win was back in 2011 at Bankstown Oval in Sydney, when we declared behind and Rene Farrell took a hat trick and changed the course of the game. The other was in Canterbury, England, in 2015, when we bowled England out in the last session on Day 4 to win the match. Celebrating with your mates after spending four days together in the field working towards something is one of my most cherished cricket memories. Especially when you get the chance to hang around in the sheds together for a while, still in your dirty whites and baggy green cap, just taking in the moment and appreciating, with great satisfaction, the toil you have all put in together.

———

The other Test that is memorable for me is the first-ever women's day/night match, which we played at North Sydney Oval in 2017. There are a number of reasons this match stands out for me, but the sense of occasion is what I remember it best for. We had the most incredible four days of support and atmosphere at the ground. The game started on a Thursday afternoon, and lots of people came down after work that day and then on Friday evening to watch the last few sessions of the day under lights. Across the weekend, it had a bit of a festival feel to it with food and drink trucks set up, music playing and people having picnics on the grass hill. There were office workers, general cricket fans, groups of young friends, families and children scattered all around the ground. Each of them enjoying the cricket for different reasons and in different ways, but all of them having equal amounts of fun.

This was the first time that I thought women's cricket had created a viable place in Australia's sporting landscape. When people turn up to watch you play, it is the most incredible reinforcement that what you have spent hours, days, years doing is worthwhile. It tells you that the way you play is entertaining, it's worthy of attention, it's something that people happily choose to spend their precious spare hours watching. Just writing this makes me smile. To know that our team is worthy of people's attention is awesome! It also makes you determined to play well and create an exciting match for people to watch. Determination can be very powerful.

In that match at North Sydney, I was really fortunate. For a few days, things went well and truly my way and I spent a bunch of time batting during our innings. I ended up

making 213 not out (after having completely embarrassed myself when I thought I had reached 200 not out before I actually did).

I'm a little reticent to write about this too much for a few reasons. Firstly, because Test matches are such a novelty in our game in comparison to the amount of limited-over cricket we play. Only two nations, Australia and England, currently play women's Test cricket, and we only play a one-off Test every few years. So, although I was truly thrilled to be personally successful in this match, many other more meaningful things have happened in the shorter format of the game. This is what each team and individual is really judged on, because ODI and T20 Internationals are the formats that we compete against every other cricketing nation in.

Secondly, I would really like to stress that the wicket we played on was an incredible batting wicket, and not many wickets were taken at all over the course of the match.

Thirdly, as great as the individual achievement was for me, we drew the Test match. So there was no real sense of accomplishment at the end of the game. Without coming across like I'm trying too hard to be modest, there was not a huge sense of fulfilment at the end of the match because there wasn't a result and it didn't add to my team's success in that series.

Having said all of that, I do want to write about the innings as well, because if there's one thing I am really proud of it's that in many ways it represents what I've tried to be as an athlete my whole career, and, more importantly, it is a strong reflection and affirmation for the thousands of hours my dad spent with me down at the nets teaching me technique, teaching me to play correctly and teaching me to value and enjoy the process of trying to perfect something.

In just about every way, the innings that I played was really my dad's. It was his influence, his incredible care and investment in my development, his amazing encouragement, support and belief in my ability, and his incredible vision and expertise about batting that played out during that match. I felt like Dad was out in the middle the whole time with me, with all the little pointers he has given me on technique replaying through my mind on repeat.

Seeing Dad at the end of the day's play, standing alongside my mum, beaming at me the way they did, is an image that I will never, ever forget. Matt and Dee were there, and close friends. That was really special.

Once I got the opportunity and I knew I had got myself in on the wicket against the English bowlers, I was determined to do it justice. A lot of it is a blur, but the one thing I remember really, really clearly is this routine that I did before every ball I faced. I don't know where it came from, because I'd never really done it before, but for whatever reason I just started to do it during that game. When the bowler was running in, I would fix my eyes on the ball in their hand and say in my head, 'Watch the ball, make good decisions.' Saying it made me so focused on that single delivery that any other thoughts I was having, of which there were many random ones, disappeared for that moment and I could just play what was in front of me.

I've kept doing this same routine ever since. It just feels right to me and gives me this total sense of clarity about what I'm doing, because it enables me to play instinctively. By that I mean that I think it enables me to play the right shot to the right ball, in the same way that my dad has taught me to do since I was five years old when we started going down to the nets.

Having those processes in place enables my body to take over and react to what's in front of it. Call it confirmation bias, but it reinforces to me that being determined to perfect something, to do it well all the time by spending lots of time practising it, at some point will pay dividends.

If you hit more cover drives well in training than you could ever care to count, then you are bound to hit them well during a match when your senses are heightened and you're totally engaged in what you are doing.

The thing is, you never know when all the practice is going to pay off, but if you believe in the process enough and have the determination to carry it through, I really do think you'll have the capacity to accomplish whatever it is that is asked of you, or whatever it is that you want to achieve.

You just need that look of determination in your eyes at the right time.

BEING
DETERMINED
TO PERFECT
SOMETHING, TO
DO IT WELL ALL
THE TIME BY
SPENDING
LOTS OF TIME
PRACTISING IT,
AT SOME POINT
WILL PAY
DIVIDENDS.

THERE'S **A CLEAR DIFFERENCE** BETWEEN **DOING SOMETHING AS WELL AS YOU POSSIBLY CAN** AND LETTING THAT **DEFINE YOU AS A PERSON.**

O ne nuance of women's cricket that might be a surprise to people is that the majority of international cricket played between countries is in limited over formats – either ODIs or T20 Internationals. In fact, the only two nations that currently play women's Test match cricket are England and Australia. Even these are quite rare, occurring only once every two years in a one-off Test match as part of a multiformat Ashes series.

The sense of occasion surrounding these one-off Test matches always seems to get people thinking about how to incorporate more Test cricket into the women's international schedule and how we can extract the absolute most out of each game in terms of it being a contest providing a great spectacle.

There are probably two things that I think of most when these discussions come up. The first is that it would be brilliant to play a similar style of series as the Ashes against other top women's cricket nations. The multiseries format that we play against England – in which there are three ODIs, one Test match and three T20 Internationals – places precedence on a team performing well in every format and is most representative of the bulk of cricket that women play at an international level. Playing a similar series against other nations would give teams the opportunity to play more Tests, while still competing against one another in the more common formats of the game.

The second thing I think of is how great it would be to have an annual home fixture during the Australian summer where the Australian Women's Cricket Team plays a Test match at the same venue on the same date each year, in a similar vain to the Boxing Day Test in Melbourne or the New Year's Test in Sydney. As I mentioned, the women's Test match held at North Sydney Oval a few years ago had a wonderful festival feel to it. While the match was the focal point, it felt like there was so much more to the event, and everyone was able to have a good time, whether they were young or old, cricket fanatic or not. It was a genuine social occasion for everyone. With an annual Test match at North Sydney Oval, people could come along, set up for the day on the grass hill or in the stands, have a picnic and/or a few drinks and watch the cricket.

The point I'm trying to make is that, when it comes to the development of our game, the sky's the limit at the moment, with an incredibly exciting group of new players coming through who will redefine the way the game is played, plus the opportunity to be innovative around the way in which we hold events and present the women's game to fans. I can't wait to see what the next few years hold!

LIKE ANYTHING, **THE MORE OPPORTUNITY WE HAVE TO PLAY TEST CRICKET,** THE MORE WE ARE GOING TO **BECOME ACCUSTOMED TO PLAYING THE FORMAT** AND, ULTIMATELY, **IMPROVE THE WAY IN WHICH WE PLAY** THE GAME.

THE
SMALL
THINGS

**THE SMALL
THINGS**

he best things! The small things are how all this started. Getting a bit addicted to the feeling of a ball hitting my bat, the feeling of running in to bowl. Lacing up a pair of boots and kicking a leather ball. Asking my parents small questions. Can we go down to the park? Can we go to the nets, please? Dad or Mum taking my brother and me down there whenever they had a spare minute, usually after a full day of work.

These small things led to other small things – my head hitting the pillow at night with me feeling as if I was still letting a ball go or hitting a few decent shots down in those nets. When you've been doing something all day as a kid, you close your eyes at night and you feel like you're still doing it. Do you know what I mean? I remember as a kid spending all day at the Easter Show on rides, and when I went to bed that night, I still felt like I was on the rollercoaster. Or you spend a whole day in the surf and that night when you're trying to get to sleep, you feel like you're still in the water. You can feel yourself going up and down in the waves all over again.

WITH SPORT, I'D CLOSE MY EYES AT NIGHT AND FEEL LIKE I WAS STILL PLAYING THE SPORT I'D BEEN DOING THAT DAY.

As a kid, the night before the grand finals of cricket or soccer, I'd dream about the game. I'd usually dream that we turned up late, because my family was notorious for being late. But before I went to sleep, I experienced that sensation of putting your head on the pillow and reliving the cricket you'd played that day, legs aching from standing on them all day long. That's how much I think you enjoy it. That's how consumed you are by it. That's how much it means to you. I still have a few nights like that every now and then.

Another small thing, a cool recent memory, is from a tour of India. India is an amazing place. There is so much energy – the people have more passion and enthusiasm than I've come across in any other part of the world. The atmosphere, the vibe, the assault on your senses can be quite intoxicating. It makes you want to embrace everything that's going on, and be swept up in what I can only describe as general madness and excitement.

We'd just finished a match and we had to do a team recovery session. Our strength and conditioning coach usually took these for us, but he had another commitment at the same time, so he entrusted us to do our own player-led recovery. Usually, recovery is a bit of an arduous task, a necessary evil that you want to complete as quickly as you can and get out of there. It was a really hot day and we all jumped in the pool back at the hotel. The standard routine is to go through some stretches, have a bit of a swim and then go back to your room. But on this occasion, we were still in the pool two hours later, as a team, everyone enjoying each other's company, mucking around, having a laugh and a cold drink. I had this unforgettable feeling of being so content with where I was and who I was with and what I was doing and how I was doing it. Something that small has become an absolute favourite memory of my time in sport.

It can be a bit of a challenge as an athlete, or in any walk of life, with all the distractions around and all the commitments we have as part of our jobs, to just stop, enjoy and take in the moment. To not be distracted by the next thing, by your phone going off or, even worse, wondering why it's not going off.

IT'S JUST **SO PEACEFUL** **TO STOP** WHERE YOU ARE AND **BE CONTENT.**

THE JOY IS
IN SEEING
HOW HAPPY
EVERYONE
ELSE IS.

Happiness is that sky-high feeling that can't stay up there forever. It's amazing while it lasts, but it's not the most sustainable of emotions. I love the feeling of contentment, or peacefulness, when you just stop thinking about everything except what is happening right in that precise moment. It's in those times that I reflect the most and think, 'I love what I do, and I'm surrounded by great people. Right now, everything is pretty okay.'

Performances aren't the be-all and end-all. Of course they're important; they're essentially the reason for training and travelling and working really hard at the way we play. When I was younger, I was meticulous about my performances at games and even at training. And maybe you have to be when you're figuring yourself out and what really matters to you. And also when you're trying to prove yourself, I guess. There were times, though, when I got too caught up in what I was doing, and it became much bigger in my own head than it really was.

There's that balance between what you're doing being really important to you in your own little world, and the fact that the outside world is not dependent on you scoring a couple of runs or taking a couple of wickets to keep spinning. It can take a while to realise, or at least to stop acting like you think it is. The fact is, the world could not care one bit.

I think I'm much more relaxed about this now, partly because I have built a lot of trust in myself and in my own processes over a lot of years. I've grown up and matured, essentially. I also have the people around me to thank – my family, my teammates – they've helped me with this a lot. They've dragged me out of that performance mindset and regularly reminded me to keep enjoying the small things.

No one has done this for me more so than my husband, Matt. It's no coincidence that I've become more successful in sport since I met him. I still work hard, but I now place greater value on the enjoyment factor, letting go of the things that were not really serving a purpose even though I thought I needed them to play well.

Ironic, isn't it, that caring a little less, and being more relaxed and trusting of my ability, has helped me improve.

THE **MOST SPECIAL KIND OF ENJOYMENT** COMES FROM THE **MOMENTS YOU SHARE** WITH OTHER PEOPLE **AND THE RELATIONSHIPS YOU BUILD.**

TO CELEBRATE
A SHARED
ACHIEVEMENT
WITH YOUR
TEAMMATES AND
YOUR FRIENDS,
NOTHING
BEATS THAT.

hen I look back at my childhood and early days in sport, I'm most reminded of the relationships. Sure, winning and being successful is fun, but it's not where the special, lifelong memories are created. They come from people and mostly happen far away from the playing field. Sport is what ties us together and creates those situations, but it's the interactions we have as people, and not as athletes, that are the most magical.

I know this sounds corny, but one of those magic moments I love is when we all crowd around together in a huddle, arm in arm, and belt out a bunch of tunes. Typically, these instances are headlined by John Farnham's 'You're the Voice'. I think I've sung that song more than any other, all over the world, in just about every kind of location. In dressing rooms, on team buses, by swimming pools, in pubs and in the middle of a cricket ground standing on a turf wicket we've just played on. It's a small thing, but standing arm in arm, looking at each other's smiling faces, singing at the top of our lungs, is just about my favourite unofficial team activity.

he real joy is in doing everything you can to have a positive impact on others around you. If you are able to help your teammates and make a difference to their day, that's so incredibly fulfilling. Taking wickets or scoring runs carries with it personal satisfaction, sure, but the real JOY is in seeing how happy everyone else is. The beauty of team sports – for better or worse – is that you're in it together, you're sharing the experiences, you're playing your different roles and you're supporting one another.

SUPPORT

he word 'support' makes me immediately think of family and friends, but also of how important it is to have the right kind of support. It sounds simple and obvious, but one of the greatest things my parents have ever done for me was to encourage me, always, to enjoy whatever I was doing. If I was enjoying it, it didn't matter to them what it was. Dad didn't take me to the nets because he was determined for me to be a cricketer. He took me there because I enjoyed it. I never felt any pressure to succeed. The joy was paramount; there was never any talk about playing for Australia or making it as a sportsperson.

One of the main reasons I play cricket – 'my why', to use a buzz phrase at the moment – or at least a huge motivating factor, is that it's always been a means for my dad and I to spend time together. Cricket has created a special bond between us. Even though I travel and play all my cricket with a big group of people that doesn't include Dad, I still spend so many hours down at the nets, sitting in a coffee shop or video chatting with him about cricket stuff. It's just our thing that we do together. Cricket is at the centre of how we relate, but it's not exactly what ties us together, either. To me, what ties us together is the fact that Dad has been there from the start. He's witnessed everything, he's supported me unfailingly, and we've shared this journey since the beginning. And I know that would be the case regardless of what I was doing – cricket, soccer or something totally unrelated to sport. Support is encouragement. Support is honesty. Support is helping your loved ones see the joy in what they're doing.

The reason I write this about my mum and dad is that I can absolutely understand how easy it can be as a parent to become overly engrossed and too invested in what their child is doing. Every parent wants to provide their child with every opportunity they can to succeed. That is completely natural. The hardest part of that is knowing

when to be involved and help, and when to pull back and let a child make their own decisions, have their own experiences and do things their own way. Even when it's really obvious that there is a better way, or more effort is needed to be successful.

One of the biggest gifts my parents have ever given me is the freedom to figure things out for myself. They've provided guidance and help at times, but they've never told me what to do. That responsibility to figure out what I want to do and how I want to do it has been mine alone. There was never any kind of reprimand when I got things wrong or didn't play well. I never had a sense that playing a bad game would disappoint Mum or Dad. I think that would have been too much for me to bear.

SUPPORT IS
ENCOURAGEMENT.
SUPPORT IS
HONESTY.
SUPPORT IS
HELPING YOUR LOVED ONES SEE THE JOY IN WHAT THEY'RE DOING.

I realise that it might sound hypocritical for me to write this, but I truly believe that sport isn't about being great at it. Sport isn't about being as driven as your parents might be.

SPORT IS ABOUT YOUR OWN PERSONAL BESTS AND REVELLING IN THE LITTLE CHALLENGES THAT COME WITH TRYING TO SELF-IMPROVE.

You don't have to be great at a sport to get great rewards. There can be just as much fulfilment in having a social hit of tennis with a friend as there is in winning Wimbledon. I recognise that's a fairly outlandish comment, but I really believe it! Sport is all kinds of things to all kinds of people. It's not just the narrow lens of performance and achievement that we often view it through.

I've always enjoyed competition, which has made it easy for me to enjoy all aspects of sport, but there is so much more to it. The social aspect of participating in a sport together and belonging to a community, the chance to be active, stay healthy, learn a new skill, just have a bit of fun.

Watching someone lift a trophy in triumph on TV is an incredibly appealing image, a dream come true for so many people. But that image doesn't portray the many things that aren't as glorious about being a professional athlete. The relentless competition, the constant judgement of your ability (and personality), the sometimes isolating thoughts about whether you're good enough, or even the inherent selfishness that comes with constantly needing to look after yourself so you can be in peak condition. For some people, experiencing those things is just not worth it, it's not enjoyable and it doesn't make them happy.

don't think you can ever push a child into being an athlete. I think that if they want to be one, they'll decide in their own good time. The greatest support a parent can provide is to make their child feel good about what they're doing.

That's not to say that there weren't times when my parents told me I needed to get out and practise. They did! But the message was never that they were disappointed in me. They could see I was getting distracted by meaningless things like binge watching TV shows... They'd tell me to go outside and kick the soccer ball. Go down to the nets. (Dad, can you come with me?) The message was never that I had to practise because I had to get better, or that the better I got, the prouder they would be of me. They encouraged me to do whatever I enjoyed and felt passionate about.

I'm conscious of the fact that a lot of the hassles athletes experience are minute compared to the battles many other people go through. I sometimes think that we become hypersensitive and overly dramatic about our challenges and issues because so many people (people who are paid to) rush to your side and pay attention to what's going on. Whether that's a reporter or a team staff member. In general terms, the things athletes have to overcome aren't usually too major.

Of course, there are exceptions, but certainly in my situation I have no grounds to speak of hardship. A couple of minor injuries, a few scratches and one or two tiny bumps in the road – I've been incredibly fortunate. I haven't had any major dramas where I've needed the sort of support you get when people rally around and drag you off the canvas. But I've had consistent support. Constant support. Whether it's something as simple as Dad picking me up from the airport whenever I've needed it, Mum always being an amazing ear and comfort for any problems, or my aunty Chris popping by for coffee, and just knowing that Matt, my parents and my friends will be there whenever I need them, the consistency of it is what has had the biggest impact on me.

Everyone around me always seems to see the best in me. I think that's the greatest support you can have.

y group of friends from school are a great example of this. We don't all spend every minute together but, in a way, it feels like we do. They probably don't know just how amazing their support has been and what it has meant to me over the years. I'm pretty sure I haven't been the best of friends at times – I've missed a lot of birthdays, other milestones and important things in their lives. In fact, I've been a terrible friend in a lot of ways. But they'll still drop everything to catch up with me when I'm home.

We laugh like we're high school girls again, chat about the silliest stuff, and, even though we've all gone on to do completely different things in our lives, our special bond remains. Without a doubt, I leave feeling lighter and happier every time I see them.

———

don't want to complain, but I don't want to make it sound like everything's been all roses either, because that's not the reality in anyone's life or job. And you can't expect it to be.

We all have our challenges and hang-ups and bad luck and frustrations and pet peeves to get past. Things don't always go our way and that's absolutely fine.

Maybe it's actually a good thing? A coach may be super-critical of you. You may be upset about something that's said. Or you're just frustrated, tired and a bit over it.

That's when it's nice to speak to people outside of the environment you're in. People who can help you see things from a different perspective. (There's that word again...)

Then you can return to your little world with a clearer idea of what you should do to get things back on track.

*It's important to recognise that
the mundane things can be
appreciated just as much, because,
without them, there wouldn't be
any rainbow at the end.*

APPRE

MILES

SHY IT'

INSPIR

BE YOU

THE H

ROSES

 ppreciation – the opposite of entitlement. Appreciating the job and situation you're in. Appreciating the people around you. Appreciating the multiple things those people do for you. And for me, appreciating this amazing lifestyle I've somehow fallen into.

Playing cricket is a love of my life, and to be able to spend this time doing it for a living is too good to be true. I'm thankful that what I loved doing as a thirteen-year-old is still the thing I'm doing more than fifteen years later.

It's easy to appreciate sitting on a beach in the Caribbean when you're playing a World Cup tournament there. Warm water, warm sun, friends – yes, I appreciate every second of that!

I APPRECIATE THE **SENSE OF FULFILMENT AND PURPOSE** THAT **PLAYING SPORT GIVES ME.**

I get complacent more often than I'd like to admit, but I try hard to not have a lack of appreciation for what I'm getting the chance to do. Catching and stopping myself when I feel like complaining about being an athlete. Travel is exciting, but it can also be tiring and often not go to plan. Hard or frustrating training sessions. Eating the appropriate food more often than not. These are all something to appreciate.

I appreciate the chance to be active every day. I feel like I've never worked a day in my life, which is another reason why I have no grounds to be providing life lessons.

━━━

I appreciate where my sport is at now versus where it's been. The fact that through fluke timing and good fortune I'm in the thick of it now. The entire landscape of women's cricket and women's sport is changing for the better. I appreciate being involved.

I appreciate the opportunities we get compared to the opportunities the players before us never had. Past Australian players had to pay out of their own pockets to represent their country. I would have done that, but the fact I don't have to – that's high on the list of things I appreciate.

For any young girl or boy who wants to play cricket for Australia, there's now a clear and visible pathway for it to happen. There's been no better time to be a young athlete, especially for young girls.

Opportunities are everywhere to get involved in sport at both a social level or, if it's of interest, as a possible career path. If it ends up the latter, then I would be the first to say what an absolutely brilliant life experience it is.

If you take up playing sport purely because you want to be involved and have fun, then I believe that's of equal value to having a professional career in sport.

To me, that is one of the greatest powers of sport – the fact that it can mean something different to everyone, and there are so many ways to derive great enjoyment and value from participating.

Sure, it might seem glitzy and glamorous to play sport at the highest level and on the biggest stage, but I think we sometimes fall into the trap of believing that's really the only level of sport with significance. We're always comparing ourselves to the best players, or speaking about how we aren't as good as one team or another. That's only representative of the top echelon of sport, where a very, very small percentage of people exist.

The real experience of sport, in my mind, is at club level, at the local park on a weekend where people come to engage in their community and play alongside friends (and, in my case, probably spend a few more dollars at the canteen than I should).

The best part about a local club is that it's available to everyone to share in the experience – it brings people together and gives us a reason to connect and have fun.

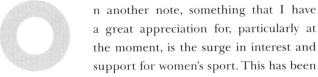O n another note, something that I have a great appreciation for, particularly at the moment, is the surge in interest and support for women's sport. This has been slowly developing for a long time, but the last few years have felt like a watershed period. I believe this reflects a recent and broader change in societal attitudes around equality and the role of women in the workplace.

In many respects, sport has led the charge for progress. With so many sports placing a priority and emphasis on increasing female involvement and leadership in their code, it fits the narrative well. Whether that's through creating a bigger platform and providing more resources for their elite female teams to compete and train, or through other avenues such as enlarging the influence and footprint of females in officialdom and executive roles, or by expanding their female fan base. In general terms, advancements that simply make sport more female friendly and easier for women to engage in.

The amount of investment that has occurred in women's team sports has, in many ways, essentially doubled the number of products that sports such as cricket can offer to the public and fans. And that's not about comparing the male and female versions of the same game and deciding which one you like to watch more. In my opinion, it shouldn't be about a comparison; rather, it should be about appreciating male and female versions of the same sport as quite different games, which can be watched with enjoyment for different reasons. At the end of the day, both variations create their own stories and their own narratives through the contest that goes on between the people on the field.

The nuances of each team, along with the way each individual plays and the various personalities of players, are unique to male and female codes of the same game. I see that people are starting to appreciate this more and more, which is incredibly exciting. Someone can be as big a fan of the Australian Men's Cricket Team as they are of the Australian Women's Cricket Team. And we certainly appreciate every single person who has shown their support!

IF YOU **TAKE UP PLAYING SPORT PURELY** BECAUSE YOU WANT **TO BE INVOLVED AND HAVE FUN,** THEN I BELIEVE THAT'S OF **EQUAL VALUE TO HAVING A PROFESSIONAL CAREER** IN SPORT.

INSPIRATIONS

usie O'Neill, I've always loved her. Roger Federer, everyone says that, but there's a reason why. And then there's Mike Hussey, the cricketer. Just the pure effort, diligence, professionalism and enthusiasm Mike had for cricket. He had to wait until he was thirty to be chosen to play a Test. His persistence was amazing. He scored 15,000 first-class runs before he even got into the Test side. Then, when he got the opportunity, he made the most of it.

I also think Tia Clair-Toomey is incredible. Not only did she win the gold medal in weightlifting at the 2018 Commonwealth Games, she has also been the World CrossFit champion three times! I can't think of a better female athlete in terms of power and speed and strength and endurance. Sheer single-mindedness and determination. Every attribute you could wish to have as an athlete, she has it. I've watched her compete a couple of times and she has some crazy kind of grit. She is truly phenomenal.

These are athletes I admire, because beyond their amazing careers there's more to them than that. They've carried themselves so well. They've seemed so sincere in their love of what they're doing. They've tried their hardest while respecting the game and their teams and their opponents.

THEY'VE BEEN **HARD COMPETITORS** BUT THEY'VE **ALSO BEEN FAIR.** THESE SORTS OF **ATHLETES INSPIRE ME.**

y real inspirations are the people closest to me. They're the people who have shaped who I am by caring so much and challenging me and encouraging me and just by being the people they are.

MY ROLE MODELS HAVE ALWAYS BEEN THE PEOPLE IN MY OWN HOME.

It can be problematic to idolise athletes or celebrities too much, because you're really only seeing their highlights. To have people close to you as role models provides a more authentic picture of how to be good. It's more raw and real and helpful and valuable. Heroes don't have to be the people who have climbed Mt Everest or won Oscars or sold a million records. They can be people close to you who are just awesome people for the sake of it, without needing fame or affirmation to feel good about themselves.

The way the people directly around you live their lives and treat other people and treat themselves – that has a bigger impact on you than someone famous who you don't really know at all.

till, I wouldn't be human if I didn't get a bit captivated by some of the overachievers. And there's one in particular: Susie O'Neill. She achieved so many amazing things as an Olympic swimmer, but what I really love is the way she went about it. She has always seemed so unassuming and shy. A beautiful human.

I've always been intrigued by people who are shy but well known, so they have to work out how to handle that. How it feels like they come out and compete and they're the centre of attention but then you can tell they just want to

TO HAVE
PEOPLE CLOSE
TO YOU AS
ROLE MODELS
PROVIDES
A MORE
AUTHENTIC
PICTURE OF HOW
TO BE GOOD.

go back into the shadows again. They're happy to be in the background. Someone else can get all the attention, they just want to do their own thing.

Susie never seemed to want to talk herself up, or talk about herself at all. As I mentioned, I read her book years ago and it's still a favourite. Reading about how she used to be petrified of her races and crippled with nerves but how she still got herself up on the blocks, and reading about how she was really shy and timid but still put herself out there in competition, there's a lot about that I admire.

I've met Susie twice and was completely starstruck both times. I sat next to her at an awards night once. We were staying at the same hotel and I spoke to her the next morning in the lobby, too. I think she noticed how overawed I was. I didn't tell her, but she could probably tell from the way I behaved. Like a babbling fan! I felt my face go bright red and I was talking too quickly, or not talking enough, or not making any sense – pretty good giveaways that I was utterly starstruck.

I was lucky enough to be at one of her world record swims – the one where she did the dance when she got out of the pool at the Olympic Aquatic Centre in Sydney. It was the first big sporting event I'd ever seen.

Susie broke the world record she always wanted and then did a bit of an embarrassed dance when she got out of the pool. I can still remember it – and I was only nine years old when it happened. She was probably too shy to know what to do, but she wanted to do something. It was a funny little dance and I loved it.

The thing is, people are people. Professional athletes are just people who have a talent and work really hard to make something of it. There are no superhuman qualities. In person, Susie was so unassuming she was almost whispering.

Now that I think of it, she matches everything that Bradman says in his quote about what we should aspire to be as Australian athletes.

INSPIRATIONS

IT'S
OKAY

IT'S OKAY

umour is a great pressure-reliever. There are always going to be moments in a game when it's intense and you're under the pump, but after the fact, if you can look back and laugh that you said this or did that, it's a powerful tool to have. Take it seriously, but not too seriously.

There have been some big World Cup matches we've lost in terrible fashion and, at the time, it feels like the end of the world. But time goes on and you realise it wasn't. There's no point crying about it forever. We sit around and say, 'Remember that time we got thrashed by such-and-such?' We all have our crappy days.

HANDLING DISAPPOINTMENT HAS BECOME EASIER WHEN I'VE LEARNED TO THINK ABOUT THE NEXT DAY, THE NEXT MATCH, THE NEXT THING ON THE AGENDA.

If you've stuffed up, as long as you learn from it, you can redeem yourself. Or we can all redeem ourselves together.

Like Mum said when I was younger, 'You've lost and you'll remember it, but no one else will. It's okay.'

---

xperiencing a disappointment gives you a good platform to get better. You can still get better when you're successful and winning, but when you lose it's a stark lesson in what you need to do to get better. Sitting on the plane on my way home, writing down in my notebook my goals, what I want to improve on next, as I do so often. The hard days, in hindsight, can end up being the most valuable days.

THE HARD DAYS, IN HINDSIGHT, CAN END UP BEING THE MOST VALUABLE DAYS.

The 50-over World Cup in 2017 was the most disappointing loss I've had. We played India in the semi-final at the County Cricket Ground, Derby. The winner would get to play England at the home of cricket, Lord's.

In the semi-final, we were totally outplayed by India in that match, and it was difficult to come to terms with that. So disappointing.

I'M A BIG BELIEVER IN A TEAM DYNAMIC THAT YOU WIN TOGETHER BUT YOU ALSO LOSE TOGETHER. THAT HELPS. THAT MAKES EVERYTHING BETTER.

You get to share the victories instead of being in this narrow little world of me, me, me. And when you're beaten, you have people you can share the pain with. There's a lot of comfort in sitting around with a group of people you've shared a goal with and being able to say, 'Well, we didn't quite get there. But there's going to be another day.'

Picking each other up. Supporting each other. There's something deep and meaningful about it that I like. The wins can feel like an out-of-body experience – but the losses are when the human qualities come through.

I'm going to remember it forever if a teammate comes over and gives me a hug and sits with me and talks to me about everything still being okay. When you win, it's euphoric and there are hugs galore, but it's easy to do. You don't even really take them in because everyone is on cloud nine and it's all a bit crazy.

A hug in a losing dressing room can sometimes mean the absolute world.

THE WINS CAN FEEL LIKE AN OUT-OF-BODY EXPERIENCE – BUT THE LOSSES ARE WHEN THE HUMAN QUALITIES COME THROUGH.

**STOP TO SMELL
THE ROSES**

golfer called Walter Hagen came up with an idea that, even if you're trying your hardest over eighteen holes of golf and the result is important, there are opportunities along the way to stop and smell the roses around the course. You're still on the course and you're still doing your job, but you can take a few moments here and there to enjoy the actual process, instead of just charging towards the end result and wanting to know what it will be. My curiosity has me wondering if Walter also came up with the concept of the 19th hole. Anyway, I agree with his idea about stopping to smell the roses.

A big precipitator to this was when I met Matt. He instilled in me that every now and then you've got to remind yourself to take a deep breath and remember there are so many worthwhile things to do and see in the world, things you don't want to miss because you're busy doing the same stuff you always do.

As an athlete, it's easy and tempting to keep chugging along looking for the next challenge, trying to get every minuscule bit out of yourself by training, preparing and competing perfectly. It might feel like the right thing to do, because your responsibility is to be dedicated to your performance. I think this is drilled into athletes from a young age, when we are surrounded by myriad people associated with sport who provide all the relevant information and science so that we can be in peak physical condition. Don't get me wrong, eating well, getting enough sleep, having good recovery practices and training well are all important, incredibly important. I've spent a good chunk of this book talking about how much I value training and putting in effort, and in my career I have leaned upon the help of many professionals associated with our team to get into the right condition to compete or to gain an advantage.

But you cannot possibly be the perfect athlete all the time, nor should you try to be. It is equally important to be able to derive joy and happiness from other things in life. In fact, it's complementary to your performance rather than detrimental.

The problem with being overly absorbed in your sport is that you might miss out on the simplest, yet most enjoyable, things in life.

There is a disconnect between enjoying the absolute highs of competing and constantly searching for affirmation and success, and being able to find appreciation and joy in things that are right in front of you every day. You can get so caught up in searching for the next achievement or accolade that you might miss out on the simple pleasure of sitting outside in the sun on a beautiful Saturday morning, reading the newspaper and enjoying a coffee.

Of course, ambition is a great thing and it's important to want to keep progressing in your career. But when you are spending time with your loved ones, looking out at a beautiful view, or when you find yourself in an ordinary situation that you might normally disregard, you should enjoy it for what it is.

There's been many a time when I've passed over these moments, and not savoured them for what they are, because I was too focused on getting to the next training session, camp or tour. But what I've learned is that they can provide just as much happiness as winning a game of sport. Sure, they are at a very different pace, but being able to change gears and jump out of the fast lane is cathartic and also really healthy. Maybe that is partly why athletes can find it so difficult to adjust immediately after they retire, because they haven't practised being in the moment during those times outside of their sport.

———

If sport is the only thing that is important, then it becomes too important. Everything in your life starts resting on it going well. To start smelling the roses, I believe you have to stop putting restrictions on yourself that only cater to you being an athlete. Having an open mind to experiences and being able to let go of your routine when it's appropriate can be liberating. In my situation, it's also made me capable of getting more out of

WHEN YOU ARE
**SPENDING TIME
WITH YOUR LOVED
ONES,** LOOKING
OUT AT **A BEAUTIFUL
VIEW,** OR WHEN YOU
FIND YOURSELF IN
**AN ORDINARY
SITUATION** THAT
YOU **MIGHT NORMALLY
DISREGARD,** YOU
SHOULD **ENJOY IT
FOR WHAT IT IS.**

myself when I am training or playing. My mind feels a lot fresher because I haven't been focused on the same thing all day long. I feel far more connected to the real world – and that makes everything seem much easier to handle.

It's also a useful tool when you are in situations that test your patience. Something like long-haul travel can be excruciating at times, especially if there are delays, you're travelling in a large group or there are long queues of people. But being agitated or annoyed at the situation doesn't make it go any quicker or even remotely fix it. Being able to turn to some teammates and have a chat and a laugh, or pull out a deck of cards and play a game, helps you pass the time in a much more enjoyable way. I've learned some cool things about teammates and support staff when sitting next to them on a plane, things that have just come up in conversation because we've been basically trapped in our seats and have had the time to talk.

THE MOMENT I'M IN SHOULD BE AS IMPORTANT AS PLANNING FOR THE MOMENTS I'M LOOKING FORWARD TO DOWN THE TRACK.

I've tried to be a lot better at smelling the roses over the last five or six years. To be able to stop in the midst of a game and take in the scenery around me, to appreciate every drop of the career I'm lucky enough to be having.

At the same time, I want to see what else is out there, to still be able to savour other things that are important to me and give me fulfilment aside from cricket. This is not something that I've managed to do overnight. It's been an ongoing process that, in part, has been a natural development as I've matured and become more experienced and comfortable with myself and my place in the team. It's also evolved because I'm conscious of trying to take in the world around me and be in the moment as often as I can.

I search for things to do in any downtime we have – like heading to a music gig, packing a picnic into a backpack and going on a bike ride for the day, stopping and chatting with locals wherever I am, and continuing the quest for good coffee in foreign cities.

I focus on anything I know I'll enjoy and what will be enjoyable to do with other people. And I try to stop myself from planning the next thing when I'm still in the middle of doing something else. Focusing solely on the present and getting the absolute most out of that experience, even if it is sitting on an airport terminal floor with a group of teammates waiting for our flight to be called.

THE BEST MOMENTS ARE THE ONES YOU DON'T KNOW ARE GOING TO HAPPEN UNTIL THEY DO.

Another part of smelling the roses is celebrating success and milestones. Our coach, Matthew Mott, is brilliant at getting the team to enjoy each other's company and to celebrate any successes we have.

Some of my favourite moments are when the game has finished and we sit on the ground we've just played on, or hang out in the change rooms for a while. After our big win at the 2018 T20 World Cup in the Caribbean, we stayed at the ground for a long time after the match. Ages. I was routinely drug-tested along with a few of the other girls – for a process that is normally quite boring, even that seemed totally glorious.

The next day, we went to a beautiful spot to have our photo taken with the trophy and then we went out to dinner as a group and hung out. We didn't do anything extraordinary, but we did everything together, and I thought that was an incredibly nice way to mark the moment.

IF YOU **DON'T STOP TO CELEBRATE MILESTONES,** YOU ARE **MERELY PASSING THE TIME.**

Opening your eyes to the world – not just your world of gyms, training fields, cricket pitches and dressing rooms, but the whole world with all its incredible diversity, beauty and craziness – makes the entire experience so much more enjoyable.

WHAT I'VE LEARNED IS THAT **A MOMENT IN THE SUN ON A SATURDAY** CAN PROVIDE **JUST AS MUCH HAPPINESS AS WINNING A GAME** OF SPORT.

AUT

HEN

TIC

AUTHENTIC

hen I'm away from sport and not doing something I have much self-belief in, I can lack self-confidence at times. Playing sport, I feel comfortable and I feel like I can be myself because I've worked at it, prepared for it, and there aren't many situations that I'm unfamiliar with. That doesn't translate to everyday life.

I'm pretty shy. I'm so bad at public speaking. I can answer questions in front of a crowd, that seems to be fine, but standing up there by myself and delivering some kind of speech, I'm the worst. I hate it.

If I have to do a speech, if there's no way I can get out of it, or if it's something I really should do, I won't sleep the night before. I'll feel ill the entire day leading up to it. I won't be able to eat if it's after a dinner, which makes things even worse. I can't breathe. I can't think straight. I forget what I'm meant to be saying. I get this incredible tightness in my chest. I take these huge gulps of air and the sentences get shorter and shorter because I keep running out of breath.

In big crowds, I don't know, I'm completely hopeless. It's horrible. I can't seem to look up when I walk into a room with lots of people there. Any kind of social situation, particularly when I'm by myself, can be a real challenge.

With people I know well, I'm fine. But otherwise, I'm so awkward. I want so much for things to not be awkward that I just make it even more awkward!

I absolutely hate confrontation – that's another trait I've come to accept about myself. There's nothing wrong with any of it. It's good to know yourself.

TRYING TO BE **PERFECT IS OVERRATED.** TRYING TO **DO YOUR BEST IS THE ACCOMPLISHMENT.**

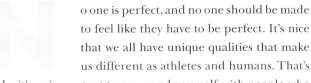

o one is perfect, and no one should be made to feel like they have to be perfect. It's nice that we all have unique qualities that make us different as athletes and humans. That's why it's so important to surround yourself with people who truly care about you.

Everyone is going to have a different opinion about you. You can't control that. I've just tried to do what's natural for me. Whether or not it works out, I can't complain because I've done it in a way that I feel good about. I haven't tried to be what everyone thinks I should be. Self-perception is the only perception that really matters. You don't have to pretend your weaknesses don't exist. They're part of who you are, they're completely normal, and once you're open about them it's easier to see what you can do about them.

I completely don't mind when friends take the piss out of me, because it says to me that they accept all my idiosyncrasies – of which I have many. It's actually one of my favourite things. And I'm more than happy to take the piss out of them in return.

I've always admired people who have this great ability to do what they do well and take it seriously, while never actually taking themselves too seriously. I think there is a great balance and outlook to find in that.

IT'S **EMPOWERING AND LIBERATING** TO ACCEPT YOURSELF FOR **WHO YOU REALLY ARE.**

here is often such a disconnect on social media between what people are pretending to be and what they really are. There's clearly no understanding that life is full of ups and downs, because when you look at a feed it can seem that everyone else is having non-stop ups.

The person you portray yourself as on social media isn't as important as the person you actually are when you're off the internet. If those two people are the same people, you're onto something.

THESE ARE **MY STRENGTHS** AND THESE ARE **MY WEAKNESSES.** WHEN YOU THROW THEM **ALL TOGETHER, YOU HAVE A PROPER PERSON.**

I love this notion of kids being 'anti-fragile' – that, by nature, children are meant to be so resilient and unstoppable and the rulers of their own world, because they haven't been exposed to everything else that goes on in the broader world. Childhood is their chance to grow and develop in their own way, as their own person, without the influence or distraction of things that they shouldn't have to know about or worry about at their age.

I think social media has dragged kids out of their own realm and into the adult world far sooner than they need to be. It's given rise to issues in relation to anxiety and depression. Of course, there is always going to be an element of those, and I'm not remotely downplaying the seriousness of mental health issues in teenagers and children. But a lot of experts are starting to say the rise in these conditions is strongly linked to the increasing presence of social media and how heavily cultivated and fake it is.

Unfortunately, kids can start to think that, as long as their life looks great on social media, who really cares what they're actually doing with their real lives. A hundred likes can make them feel great about themselves. Not enough likes can make them feel unliked or that they're a failure.

There's too much pressure to impress, to get likes.

Social media doesn't show what people's lives really are. You're comparing all your mundane stuff to other people's highlights – they look like they're forever on the beach, or on holidays, or having amazing adventures, all the while living life with the most incredible discipline and dedication to their diet and fitness. I think it's just about being able to decipher between what is a genuine depiction and what is a distorted or idealised picture of reality.

I can't say I've had any bad experiences with social media because, to be honest, I hardly ever use it. If there's been nastiness directed at me, I've most likely missed it. There are better things to do in the real world. If there's drama on social media, it can start to dominate your life – where's the sense in that?

I'm not trying to preach to anyone to not be on social media. There is certainly some good in it if it's used well and you're connecting with people you really want to connect with. There's a great benefit in having a close-knit group of people who stay in touch on social media, the friends who you catch up with regularly in real life, so there's none of the pressure to try to impress each other. There are also people and organisations worthy of attention, those who use social media in a way that creates positivity and provides inspiration and motivation to a lot of people.

How I play sport and how I interact with people in real life is more important to me than trying to post a witty comment with a photo. It's also a fair bit harder to be good at that. I'd prefer to be judged by the way I carry myself on and off a sporting field, how I respond to life in the moment. Hopefully I do that well enough.

As athletes, it's our responsibility to do the right thing by the people who choose to support our team, and we really value that support. However, I do believe there is a fine line between expressing your appreciation and allowing athletes to maintain an element of privacy. Social media has blurred that line even more, as everyone is much more accessible and to a higher personal degree. The expectation about what you should share and when you can be contacted has gone to a whole new level.

What I'm trying to express is that I know I have actively made the decision to engage in public life through playing sport – and I hope that is how I can have an impact on society in a positive way – but I don't want to compromise the things that are sacred to me and the people who are close to me by creating an online image of myself that isn't authentic or that covers up all the flaws I have.

I'D MUCH RATHER SHOW **THE REAL VERSION OF ME,** WHICH IS **FAR LESS SPECTACULAR THAN THE VIRTUAL VERSION,** BUT ACTUALLY **BETTER AND MORE MEANINGFUL** BECAUSE IT'S **AUTHENTIC AND IMPERFECT.**

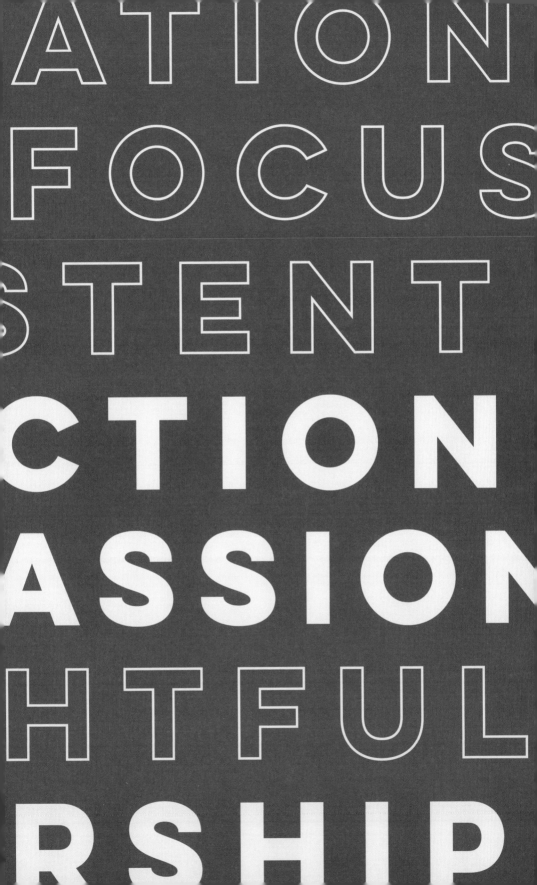

MUSIC

ne of my favourite things is to go to live music shows. You watch someone perform and it's like they're pouring their heart onto the stage and saying, 'Here you go. This is who I am, this is who we all are as humans'. We have a lot of shared experiences and emotions and we should celebrate all of them, all the heartaches as well as the triumphs. It's all part of being alive.

I admire musicians – basically anyone who knows how to blow a note on a trumpet or any instrument – because if I could be anything in this world, it would be a musician. They just have this incredible ability to connect with people in concerts, in their songs, in their lyrics. They connect with our emotions and become a part of our lives. They're in the car with us when we're playing their music. They're at parties with us when we put their tunes on in the background. They're in our heads when we're humming or singing their songs all day. That amazes me.

We can have this deep, personal connection with musicians, even when we don't know them personally. It's mind-blowing the impact they have.

You see people in the audience and they're bawling or they've got goosebumps or they look overjoyed because it's a song that means something to them. It might bring back memories, good or bad, or it might make them feel optimistic about the future.

Thousands of people at a concert can have these incredibly deep, personal moments at the same time, but each one of those moments is unique. I look at this one person on a stage and think about what he or she has contributed to people's lives and I'm in awe of the creativity and self-expression and the boldness of it.

A song comes on that everyone recognises and it's this explosion in the room of pure elation. Magic. I can't imagine what that sort of response must feel like to the performer, to be up there on stage, singing their song and seeing people being swept away by it.

The song might have just started as a little idea in their mind. They might have scribbled down a few words on a piece of paper or in a notebook of their own.

They've come up with a tune in their bedroom and then they get to the stage and the words come from their mouth and their lungs, or a tune comes from the strings of their guitar, and the audience starts screaming because they love it so much.

I wonder if they know how profound the effect is.

Probably because I'm so tone deaf and terrible at music, musicians are the people who fill me with awe. The smaller gigs are the ones I love; they're more intimate than the big stadium shows.

THOUSANDS OF PEOPLE AT A CONCERT CAN HAVE THESE INCREDIBLY DEEP, PERSONAL MOMENTS AT THE SAME TIME, BUT EACH ONE OF THOSE MOMENTS IS UNIQUE.

MOTIVATION

ntrinsically, I'm quite motivated. I like watching sports documentaries and life documentaries. I like reading, fiction and non-fiction. I find those kinds of stories interesting and they're very important in terms of broadening my thinking and re-emphasising the fact that there are many different activities to do in this world and many ways of doing them. Sometimes, one might spark a new thought for me that I'll follow up, or enable me to learn about something that I might be oblivious to because of being stuck in my own world and with my own ways of doing things.

I don't think, however, that I deliberately watch shows or read to find motivation and inspiration. That's not to say that I don't find other people or their circumstances inspirational. It's that, most of the time, my motivation comes from within. In large respect, that's because I believe that if your motivation comes from within yourself it's always going to be there. Sure, your motivation may wane or falter at times, but deep down you'll always be able to find it and call on it.

Reading a great book or watching someone's life story may help you to get revved up, of course, and you can feel inspired, but you can't hold onto that feeling forever.

In the end, you're there on your own and you're the one who has to make the call to take the initiative.

———

love the consistent feeling of satisfaction when I've finish a training session. Maybe it's because I'm someone who's drawn to consistency, and I also like the idea of turning up for training because you're motivated to get better, to push yourself, to learn something new without the need for affirmation from a crowd or for numbers on a scoreboard. The internal drive to spend your time doing something worthwhile every day, something to evaluate yourself on, to chip away at and be satisfied with when you head home for the evening.

The other thing about training is that you are entirely in control. You can dictate what you want to work on, how hard you want to push yourself, how determined you want to be to improve or learn. In a match, there's much that's out of your control. That in itself makes playing exciting and worth throwing yourself into but, for me, it doesn't provide the same sense of consistent satisfaction that finding intrinsic motivation at training does.

My love of work and training doesn't for a second mean that I don't have days where my motivation wavers. At times, I can easily think of other things I would prefer to be doing, or I wish that training would hurry up and finish so I can get home or do something different. That happens to me, as I'm sure it does to just about everyone else at various times. But the one thing I always come back to is that I know for a fact I've never not felt better about things once I've just got stuck in and done the work I need to do. At the very least, the fitness session, weights session or team session I was dreading is never, ever as bad as I envisaged it would be before starting out.

THE MOST IMPORTANT THING, AND MAYBE THE HARDEST, IS TO JUST START.

Once you're going, it's amazing how quickly your body and mind snap into gear and you begin enjoying it.

With training and working as hard as you can, it's entirely up to you. Essentially, it's inherently self-motivated because there's no crowd there watching and cheering you on. There are no immediate rewards, trophies, TV cameras or media waiting to write about you and what you did. There isn't any kind of fanfare at all.

There always are, however, the people you play with, and the coaches and support staff who help you prepare. Knowing that you can have a direct effect on a teammate and her training, potentially impacting how much she enjoys it, and that there might be an opportunity to work together to figure something out, is also motivating.

On a particular day, if you're struggling to be in it for yourself, you can always be in it for someone else, and in a team sport you should be.

One of the best things about training with someone else is the fact that you have a responsibility to them. If I plan to do a training session on my own and then go to bed that night later than I wanted to, or I wake up feeling rubbish, there's a much bigger chance I'll put off training or not do it at all. But if I know I've organised to meet someone and they are relying on me to turn up for the session, I won't want to let them down or leave them hanging. It's also brilliant to share those sessions that you're battling through a bit with someone else. It's amazing how most of the time you'll find they're on the same page, or if you're competitive you end up wanting to match their standard and that, in a sense, pulls you out of your funk.

In writing all this, I'm not for a minute suggesting that any particular type of inspiration is the right or the wrong kind. What I do think, though, is that it's important to be aware of where your motivation comes from. I think I've gained an understanding of what gets me most excited to do things or, to use a cliche, what gets me out of bed in the morning.

But that doesn't mean that, if you're someone who's motivated more by the attention, the performance rewards from playing a match or by someone's achievements, it's a bad thing. It's equally important, it just means that you may need to shape the way you train, prepare and do the things necessary to get those rewards. As long as you find a way to largely enjoy what you do, day in and day out, it really doesn't matter where your motivation comes from.

My view on motivation is this – when you strip it all back, it's just you, the people you work alongside and a choice. You can choose to either work as hard and as smart as you can, knowing that will lead towards some kind of deep personal satisfaction, or just cruise through it and tick a box but not necessarily gain anything particularly tangible. And the best person to decide which way to go is you.

PASSION

ard work isn't the right word for what I do. Cricket training, the net sessions and fitness work is so enjoyable to me that there's nothing I really dislike about it. I embrace all of it. Of course, there are frustrations and disappointments, losses and wrong decisions, moments I'd like to have over again.

But when you've found your passion and you're doing it because you love it, you put up with the downtimes because you want to keep doing it. You want to keep going. You're so fascinated by it that you can't help doing it.

FOR ME, THAT'S BEING AN ATHLETE. THAT'S WHEN I FEEL MOST LIKE MYSELF.

It doesn't matter what you're doing. If you get that feeling from business or music or art or teaching or photography or whatever makes you feel passionate – we're all on the same page. There are so many life lessons to be shared.

Crafting a career and going all-in and discovering what works for you and taking your opportunities, it's the same for everyone, in every field.

How can someone become a better school teacher? Or barista? The same way that someone can become a better cricketer. Continually trying to evolve.

It sounds corny, perhaps, but I think there's so much beauty in working away at something, being consistant in the attempt, continuously building your skills and experiences, and giving yourself a bigger and bigger foundation to grow.

It's not always easy to see the beauty in the work phase and it probably comes in hindsight, to a degree. But it's there. You can be hating a particular session but there's still a voice deep down inside you thinking, 'I love this'. If I didn't love cricket, I don't see how I could devote myself to it.

Four of the best words in the English language – do what you love.

As a career.

If that's not possible, as a hobby.

---

raining, for me, is like being at school again, learning as much as possible and getting better, keeping your eyes and ears open. The game is the examination. How much have you learned? Have you done the work you were meant to do? Each year, as you grow up, the exams get a little bit harder and the tests become more serious. If you haven't done the study, the practice, you're not going to pass the exam, perform in the match. The more little areas of expertise you have, the more likely it's going to serve you well when a few tricky questions are thrown in.

THE **THRILL OF SPORT** IS THAT **THERE ARE** **STILL NO GUARANTEES.**

If you've nailed your study for a school exam, you can walk in almost knowing you'll pass. You deserve to. In sport, you can study like crazy but the match might still not go your way. Someone who isn't really prepared can come in and play well.

But the more you've studied, the more likely you are to do well, and do well consistently. At some stage, you will get what you deserve in sport. You end up doing enough exams that you know what you need to do beforehand to pass them. That's how it feels to me.

Study hard. Work hard. Get prepared. See how you go.

The thought of the exam or match can be daunting, but knuckling down to get ready for it feels doable. So that's what you do. You don't worry about anything except the study until the exam comes along. You get into the exam and you realise, 'Oh my goodness, I know more than I thought!' Or if there are areas of a game in which you've struggled, you know what you have to go back to and work on. I sometimes enjoy the feeling of being in school again more than the feeling of doing the exam on the field.

The harder you practice, the luckier you get.

I GET **PASSIONATE ABOUT THE CRAFT, BUT I DON'T WANT THE WHOLE EXPERIENCE** TO **HINGE ON THE RESULTS.**

HIGH
PERFORMANCE

am passionate about taking the opportunity we have as a team to help our sport evolve and grow. The profile of women's cricket is rising so quickly.

A great example of this is that the final of next year's home T20 World Cup will be held at the Melbourne Cricket Ground. What an amazing opportunity, especially given that the ground holds around 100,000 people and the aim is to hopefully fill the stadium. What an opportunity for women's cricket to be on one of the biggest sporting stages in Australia.

This growth is the end result of all the training and the high-performance things you implement along the way. You spend more time training than you do competing. Attempting to turn all those sessions into a performance at the highest level, that's the riddle we're all trying to solve.

IT'S ABOUT HAVING A PURPOSE TO EVERY WORKING DAY. A FOCUS. SOMETHING YOU'RE TRYING TO ACHIEVE.

If you don't get there, it doesn't matter. You can try again the next day. The important thing is to be making the effort. Having a reason to get moving every day.

oals are good. Small goals. Personal goals. Continually trying to evolve or find a better way. I believe there are always ways to do things better, but I just don't know them, yet. So I want to go looking for them. I want to train.

Exploring the boundaries around training is probably the one part of me that is creative. The idea that there's always more I can do. I'm no good at art, I wish I was good at music – I'm not even close – but in sport I really like the idea of getting creative around the physical training.

Just because you've done something one way for a long period of time, doesn't mean you can't go out and find new ways or new answers. You can try anything once. If it doesn't work, it doesn't work and you can go back to what you were doing before. Nothing's been lost.

There's a quote about how if you're not trying to change the game, you're playing someone else's game. It's in my notebook and increasingly in my thoughts:

> 'THERE'S **NO LIMIT** ON THE WAY YOU CAN **EXPLORE YOUR OWN TALENTS** AND CAPABILITIES.'

High performance has certainly become more prominent in the last few years in sport, or at least it is spoken about a lot more, and most teams or organisations have high-performance managers who oversee all their processes. High performance is a broad church of ideas and concepts that encompasses so much in relation to elite sport. It can be about training methods, program structures, scheduling, leadership, coaching methods, culture, group dynamics – a wide range of concepts that all impact performance.

All these different aspects have the ability to provide you with an advantage if you do them well. This means it's every ambitious team's goal to be world-leaders in the practice of high performance. And these concepts are continually evolving and changing as various organisations invest time and money in figuring out the best way to do things, constantly trying to find an edge, a key to success.

COMBINING HIGH LEVELS OF SKILL WITH HIGH LEVELS OF ATHLETICISM IS ONE OF THE GREATEST ADVANTAGES YOU CAN HAVE AS AN ATHLETE.

It won't be particularly surprising that the question about what's the best way to train and prepare fascinates me when it comes to cricket. I'm not talking solely about the skills of the game – batting, bowling and fielding – but much more broadly about how can we create the very best athletes whose physical attributes are most suited to playing the game of cricket and also make them much better at cricket than they would be without those attributes. In this sense, I think there are things that other sports do really well that cricket typically doesn't do as well, and where we could learn quite a lot.

In part, this is because there are some traditional aspects of cricket that dictate the way we train. For example, I don't think the typical structure of a net session has changed since the very beginning of net sessions. Also, I think there's been an emphasis and attitude from a lot people involved in cricket that it's a skills-based sport, so physical conditioning and athletic qualities are far less important than being highly skilled as a batter or a bowler. Therefore, some believe we shouldn't spend much time on physical conditioning. There is logic in this, and I am in absolute agreement that being highly skilled at what you do is hugely important and that you aren't going to get very far as a cricketer without those skills.

However, I would argue that being fitter makes you even better at your skill, because becoming physically strong and efficient in movement delays the onset of fatigue, meaning you are able to execute skills for longer, produce the skills more powerfully and do so at a quicker pace.

Combining high levels of skill with high levels of athleticism is one of the greatest advantages you can have as an athlete; it's imposing to the opposition, by making you appear relentless, and has the capacity to produce mental and physical fatigue in your opponents.

believe we can learn from other sports that are, perhaps, more advanced than cricket in terms of valuing athletic development as well as skill acquisition. For instance, a big part of the football codes is robust running. Being able to run efficiently, quickly and technically well with a ball in your hand, while also knowing that at some point someone is going to try to tackle you.

Most of the time, a cricketer has something in their hand, the ball or bat, or is trying to catch or pick the ball up in the field.

TO BE ABLE TO MOVE EFFICIENTLY WHILE THOSE CONSTRAINTS ARE OCCURRING MAKES YOU CAPABLE OF HAVING MORE OF AN IMPACT ON THE GAME.

If you can run and turn quickly between wickets, you're capable of scoring more runs for the team. If you can get to the ball faster in the field, you're potentially going to cut down the number of runs the opposition scores. If you run up to the wicket in a more balanced, efficient fashion, you are going to most likely be more balanced delivering the ball when bowling.

I believe in the notion of training around something as specific as those actions. There's no point running just for the sake of running, or lifting weights just for the sake of lifting weights. That to me is boring and demotivating. But if you know you're doing a running session that is going to directly help you score more runs in a game and challenge the opposition, there are so many reasons to turn up to that session.

Similarly, by developing strength in the parts of your body that are the same areas you use when you're batting, and then combining that improved strength with good batting technique, you're going to be able to hit the ball harder and further than you otherwise could. That's a really cool reason to turn up to the gym before, or after, you've spent time in the nets.

The other point about this notion of athletic development is that it makes the game more exciting to watch. Every fan appreciates watching athletes who are not only highly skilled but also supremely athletic. Games are played at a faster pace and are more dynamic.

━━━

n writing all this, I don't by any means profess to know all the answers – I don't have a degree in sports science, I haven't studied high performance.

But I think there is more than enough evidence available and good reasons to keep evolving to find the best training methods and practices for cricket.

A cricket team has eleven different personalities and eleven different techniques and eleven different attitudes but, more often than not, only one way of training. At the end of the day, we're playing the one sport and there's uniformity there. But having different people coming from different perspectives can be refreshing.

That's where I think Australian women's cricket has an incredible opportunity. The professional era is very, very new to our sport, and so there are few ingrained practices or cultural barriers to the way we train – we are a relatively blank canvas, so to speak. At the moment, we often follow the male system's blueprint and practise as a guide because those are pre-existing. But there is enough nuance and difference between male and female athletes to consider tailoring our training to suit female athletes better. We could take this chance to experiment and, potentially, provide evidence or set new standards for the way all cricketers can do things.

In the years to come, and maybe this is overly ambitious, it would be amazing to see us set the standard for high-performance practices across the board for female sport, both in Australia and around the world.

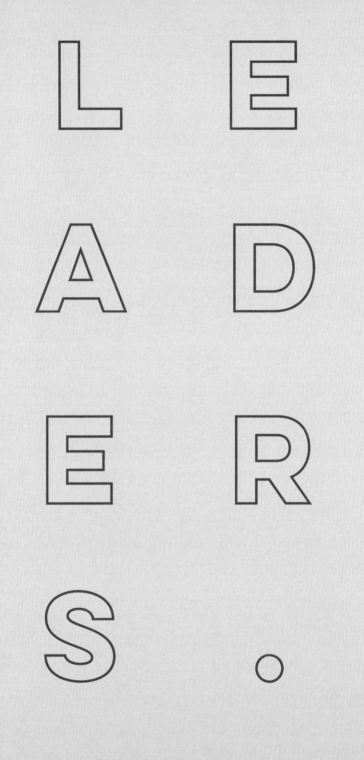

LEADERSHIP

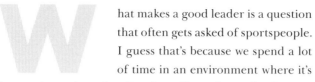

hat makes a good leader is a question that often gets asked of sportspeople. I guess that's because we spend a lot of time in an environment where it's key to give and receive direction efficiently. Leadership can be quite an abstract concept to talk about – there is no exact science when it comes to leading a group of individuals who, by nature, are unique and unpredictable. Some people spend a lot of time studying exactly which leadership characteristics are important or will have the most impact.

I have a few observations, as they relate to sporting, that I think are central components of leading a team – both in a formal capacity, such as being a captain or vice-captain, as well as more informally. I'd like to stress that I definitely don't have all the answers about this topic, and I'm not considering a whole gamut of other factors and theories that can impact leadership. I haven't spent anywhere near enough time pondering the answers, nor have I done a huge amount of leadership training.

THE BEST LEADERS I'VE SEEN ARE THE ONES WHO LEAD NATURALLY AND AUTHENTICALLY.

That is, they do it in their way and their own style, not by trying too hard to be someone they're not. They have a natural manner and flair about them, as well as particular leadership strengths that draw people towards them.

Some are great leaders by the example they set – the hardest worker, the best player, the most talented or conscientious. Others have tremendous interpersonal skills and emotional intelligence, which make people want to listen and be on a journey with them, as they always seem to gauge the mood correctly and say the right things at the right time.

If someone possesses both sets of qualities, they can be truly inspirational leaders.

As role models, inspiring leaders show you the way by excelling and performing in the same environment as you do, and they are also able to express a level of empathy and vulnerability that makes them human and on the same level as you. You're not afraid to ask them questions, learn from them and, importantly, develop a friendship that means you know them as a person and not solely as a figurehead.

I often think this kind of leadership shows up best in tough times, if you have to engage in an uncomfortable conversation with one another, or when people are being challenged and need resilience for situations that aren't going well, or not going the way they would want them to.

GENUINELY WANTING TO SUPPORT EACH OTHER BECAUSE YOU KNOW THERE IS A LEVEL OF CARE THAT EXTENDS FAR OFF THE PITCH IS POTENTIALLY ONE OF THE MORE POWERFUL TOOLS A TEAM CAN HAVE.

Developing an encouraging, supportive and thoughtful culture takes the involvement of more than just one or two leaders, although it can certainly start with them. If the most influential people in the team set the standard, and express their values well, their guidance can have an incredible impact on the rest of the group.

While the results may not flow immediately, I do believe it will put you all on a path to long, sustainable success, because you truly enjoy sharing the good times together, while embracing and weathering any storms that may hit along the way.

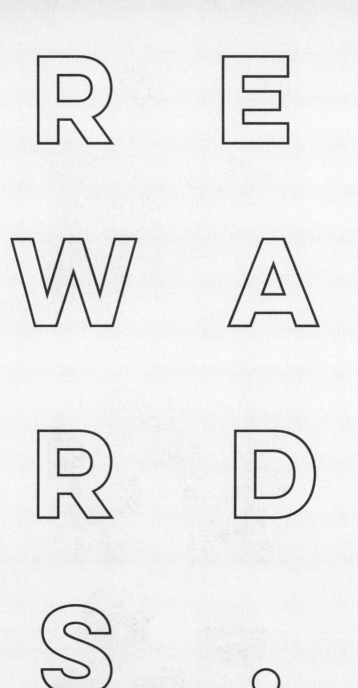

REWARDS AND
REFLECTION

f you asked me as a twelve-year-old what my ideal reward was for anything I did, it would have been, without a doubt, getting an ice cream from the service station on the way home. I would have been chuffed with that and, honestly speaking, Dad was often far too obliging. He properly spoiled my brother and me on plenty of afternoons after school, or on the way home from sport on the weekend.

Having the odd ice cream still tickles my fancy, but now my concept of rewards is a lot more abstract and intangible than it used to be when I was a kid. I feel guilty when I think about all the rewards I've received for doing something that I love, to the point where I don't believe I'll ever be able to reconcile myself with the fact that I have been so incredibly fortunate and been afforded so many amazing things in my life. The rewards for all my 'toil' have been an incredible lifestyle, so many special people being in my life, a lifetime of experiences from around the world, and a platform like this book to share my opinions on things.

Where I am in my career now is a reflection of every single ball my dad has thrown to me in the nets over the last twenty years. That's how I would sum it up. Maybe a reward for our toil. Twenty years of Dad throwing balls to me comes together when I walk onto the pitch with my teammates to represent Australia.

But we never knew during those twenty years that there would be more than 200 games I'd get to play for Australia as a result. We went through those twenty years on a day-by-day basis. What I'm trying to say is you never know where it might lead when you just keep plugging away at what you love.

NINETY PER CENT OF YOUR TIME AS AN ATHLETE IS SPENT PREPARING TO COMPETE.

I think of the invisible hours – the ones that most people don't see. The hours that are the most crucial of all. Hitting a miracle shot under pressure when you just have to make it isn't really a miracle. You're just hitting the same shot you've hit a thousand times before, but you're doing it at a miraculous time. The shot that can win a T20 match on the final ball isn't something you've pulled out of the hat at the last minute. It's the exact same shot you've hit for invisible hour after invisible hour.

For me, in a way, the hours spent training are the most enjoyable hours. They're the hours that give me the confidence to go out and play. A game only lasts so long. You might only bat for one ball. In T20 matches, we bowl only four overs. Look at Usain Bolt. All the preparation he does for a performance that goes for less than ten seconds.

The invisible hours with Dad. The invisible hours now. I don't think I've changed. We still go down there together. I still ask him the same question, the question lots of kids ask every summertime: 'Dad, can we go down to the nets?' I still get such a buzz from heading down there and hitting cricket balls, the crack sound on the bat, the feeling of getting it right and having every part of your body in balance and in the right position to hit a certain shot. Then trying to do it again. And again.

THE INVISIBLE HOURS
ARE SO PURE BECAUSE THEY'RE **SOLELY FOR SELF-IMPROVEMENT.**

Every ball is its own entity, if that makes sense. A cricket ball is a cricket ball. It doesn't know who's delivered it. It doesn't know who's about to hit it.

Training sessions are so freeing because there's no result to tell you whether you've succeeded or failed. It's all about the feelings the sport gives you. You're not trying to beat anyone else. There are no losers, so all you can do is win.

There have been lots of important people along the way, and Dad and Mum are the ones who've been there since day one. And I know they'll stay there long after I stop. In terms of my career, I'm really glad I've been able to do some things for them. Not that they have ever, ever expected it of me. But I don't think they realise just how much they've done and continue to do. Mum's hug on the boundary line after a game is still the most comforting and warm feeling in the world. The most overwhelming and rewarding feeling I'll ever experience is seeing the smiles and joy that crosses their faces every time I see them at our matches.

was about six years old when Dad and I started doing training together. I was always reasonably coordinated, with the emphasis on reasonably, but any success I've had is definitely from the work I've put into it. You have no idea how many balls I've hit. Just Dad and me down there, ball after ball. I don't know how his arm didn't fall off.

Because we've done it so often, it feels like a normal part of my life. There's never been any huge leaps of improvement, I don't think. It's just been this gradual progression in getting my act together. Do it once. Do it again. And again. Until it becomes automatic.

You know when you don't see someone for six months and you think, wow, they've changed? It makes me think of that.

If you saw me as a young cricketer from day one to six months later, you might have thought, 'Jeez, she's so much better!' But to me, I hadn't really changed at all. When you're doing it every day, you don't realise how far you've come along. It's just one step at a time.

When Dad needed to start chasing the balls because I'd hit them past him, and when he went back and started throwing balls from the full length of the pitch, that's when I probably began to feel like a cricketer. Initially, he had been halfway up the pitch, doing little under-arms to me.

I can remember my first bat so clearly, more clearly than most of the bats I've owned since – it was a size 3 Kashmir Willow Gray-Nicolls. My first proper bat was a Gunn &

Moore Maestro. Oh, I loved that bat! Oiling it. Knocking it in when it was brand new by putting a ball in a sock and hanging the sock from the clothesline. I can still see the stickers on all my bats, the shapes of them, the feel of them in my hands, how they felt when I put my feet shoulder-width apart and took my stance, how the ball felt and sounded coming off them.

———

Bradman's quote, which I shared at the beginning of this book, encapsulates the values that I think are important and how I think sport should be played. You can be competitive and determined and you can do everything in your power to do well but you can also be content with just knowing what you've done within yourself, and not need to tell everyone about it and blow your own trumpet and be flamboyant or arrogant or lacking in grace.

I love that idea of succeeding at sport while still trying to be a nice human being. That's the best way I can be true to myself. The perfect state would be to have a level of contentedness within myself that means that winning or losing doesn't have any impact on my sense of self-worth. That's not always easy in sport – it's such a results-based business. Winning is part of what you're getting paid to do. And there are times I get determined around things. There's a way to win and lose and still be a nice human being regardless of what happens in a sporting contest.

Being an athlete is an incredibly selfish vocation, and there are days when I'm single-minded about what I want to achieve. Sometimes, in those self-absorbed states, you don't realise how much you are just ploughing through things without appreciating anything or anyone around you. It's only later you think, 'Oh wow, I've had Metallica playing in my head the whole day.' But if you have some kind of conscious awareness of it later on, it's probably okay.

Most of my favourite interactions with people have nothing to do with sport, anyway. They're about life.

FAR AWAY FROM ANY SPORTING FIELD, WHERE THE **REAL AND TRULY TANGIBLE THINGS IN LIFE OCCUR,** I THINK THAT'S WHERE **YOU GAIN THE MOST AS A PERSON.**

Bradman makes me think of all that. How multi-faceted he was. He could play the piano and he was intelligent, and he was close to his wife but he was also the greatest cricketer who ever lived. I admire that he was anything but one-dimensional. He seemed to have core principles that he was quite unwavering about. Bradman, the greatest ever cricketer, was more than a cricketer.

don't want to be a human being who's defined solely by what I do as an athlete. There's got to be more to me than that. I really, really want there to be. I want to love the scenery around me. I'm obsessed with sunrises and water and a beautiful patch of grass – anything that reminds me of how lucky we are to be here. A sunrise – what a way to appreciate a day, to actually see it being born. Fresh air, as silly as that sounds. An amazing cup of coffee. Interactions with people. Those are the things in this world that make me stop in my tracks.

When you're standing on the boundary in a game of cricket and someone has a chat to you over the fence like you're a couple of neighbours catching up on a Sunday morning. 'Hi.' 'Hi! How's it going? What do you think about the game?' They might tell you a joke. Something silly. Just the interaction is nice.

With my teammates, there are so many cheeky moments when someone says something hilarious and it puts you in a good mood for the whole match. The TV cameras often don't capture those moments.

Something as simple as another person waving you into a gap in traffic, smiling as they do it. That feels like a little victory for humanity to me. I know it sounds fairly lame, but as life become faster and faster I think we've missed those moments that signify we are all on this planet together to cooperate and enjoy life.

That's my perspective on things at least.

f I were to reflect about what's happened in my life so far, there would be many things that have made me happy, things that have made me proud, and things that I'll cherish for a lifetime.

There are also plenty of things that I've done poorly, people I should have treated better at various times, and days when I've been far from my best.

All of this has occurred at sporting fields, as well as far, far away from them. The point I'm trying to make is that we are all a work in progress, and I'm pretty certain I'll never be a finished product either.

But, hopefully, my perspective keeps evolving, and I keep learning, so I can be the best I can be.

227

THANK YOU

To Matt, for knowing me better than I know myself, for your cheekiness and making me laugh, and for always encouraging me, especially when I lack confidence.

To my very loving and caring family: Mum, Dad and Damien, and the wider Perry clan – the Princis, the Tognettis, the Mitchells, Nanna and Poppa, Nanna and Grandad, and the To'omuas. Thank you for your acceptance, generosity and support at all times.

To everyone I have shared a sports field with as a kid or adult, thank you for your mateship and for making it an amazing experience that has always given me so much joy.

My teammates and support staff at the Sydney Sixers, New South Wales, Victoria, Loughborough and Australia, thank you for tolerating my terrible jokes and annoying habits. Especially to Midge, who has had to deal with it the longest. And to my past teammates and staff in both cricket and soccer.

Jodie Hicks, for manning the fort with aplomb and always being up for a coffee at SML.

All the coaches I've had along the way, and in particular to Simon Breen, Bernie Freeburn and Greg Dwyer – you were my first-ever club team coaches and each of you always made sure that the environment was fun and enjoyable for every kid in the team, exactly the way sport should be.

To Nathan, Ben and Dean, thanks for letting me be one of the boys!

Alicia, Gi, Jacqui, Aimee, Annabel, Bec, Catrina, Clem, Clare – can we please get coffee again soon?

My Pymble and Beecroft Primary School friends and teachers – my school years will always be one of my most cherished times, because all of you made it so special and taught me so much.

To Trish, for the same wavelength, for not getting sick of my company and for reigniting the sense of adventure and wonder that I thought I had lost. Here's to sharing far more sweet and savoury, all around the world.

Josh White, Millie Dawson and all the team at Lampoon Group.

Will Swanton, for helping to tell my story.

To everyone who has ever come along to a game or watched on TV, especially the young girls and boys, or if you've written a note, stopped to say hi or hung around for an autograph after a game – it's incredible to have your support, and it means the world to all of us.

And finally, to you, for reading this book – thank you for your interest, I'm so incredibly fortunate.

HarperCollins*Publishers*
First published in Australia in 2019
by HarperCollins*Publishers* Australia Pty Limited
ABN 36 009 913 517
harpercollins.com.au

HarperCollins*Publishers*
Level 13, 201 Elizabeth Street, Sydney, NSW 2000, Australia
Unit D1, 63 Apollo Drive, Rosedale, Auckland 0632, New Zealand
A 53, Sector 57, Noida, UP, India
1 London Bridge Street, London, SE1 9GF, United Kingdom
Bay Adelaide Centre, East Tower, 22 Adelaide Street West, 41st Floor, Toronto, Ontario, M5H 4E3, Canada
195 Broadway, New York, NY 10007

A catalogue record for this book is available from the National Library of Australia
ISBN: 978 1 4607 5808 3 (hardback)
ISBN: 978 1 4607 1184 2 (ebook : epub)

Project manager: Barbara McClenahan
Art direction, cover design and internal design by Hazel Lam, HarperCollins Design Studio
Cover image © Stuart Miller Photography
Layout and typesetting by Jane Waterhouse

All photographs are courtesy of Ellyse Perry and her family, except as noted.
page ii: © Stuart Miller Photography; 3: Day 4 of the Women's Test match, Australia vs. England, Taunton, 21 July 2019 (Harry Trump/Getty Images); 10–11: shutterstock.com; 16: Sir Donald Bradman (News Ltd); 34–35: WNCL Final, NSW Breakers vs. Victoria Spirit, Sydney Cricket Ground, 25 January 2009 (Matt King/Getty Images); 48: image supplied by McGrath Foundation; 52 (top): AFC Women's Asian Cup Semi-Final, Australia vs. North Korea, Ho Chi Minh City, 5 June 2008 (Hoang Dinh Nam/AFP/Getty Images); 52 (bottom): ICC Women's World Cup, Australia vs. New Zealand, North Sydney Oval, 8 March 2009 (Tim Clayton/Corbis via Getty Images); 63: © Stuart Miller Photography; 75: Chloe Paul; 80–81: Southern Stars training session, Sydney, 30 October 2014 (Mark Metcalfe – CA/Cricket Australia via Getty Images); 98–99: ICC Women's World Twenty20 Final, Australia vs. New Zealand, Barbados, 16 May 2010 (Emmanuel Dunand/AFP/Getty Images); 102: Ellyse as a flag bearer on the day of Steve Waugh's iconic ton, when he equalled Don Bradman's 29 Test centuries, Sydney Cricket Ground, 3 January 2003; 106: Match 2 of the Rose Bowl series, Australia vs. New Zealand, 22 July 2007, Darwin (Quinn Rooney/Getty Images); 112–113: Sydney FC W-League training session, Sydney, 10 October 2012 (Phil Hillyard/Newspix); 118: © Stuart Miller Photography; 126: after scoring 213 runs not out on Day 3 of the Women's Test match, Australia vs. England, North Sydney Oval, 11 November 2017 (Mark Evans/Getty Images); 130–131: Australian Women's Cricket training session, North Sydney Oval, 7 November 2017 (Mark Kolbe/Getty Images); 140–141: shutterstock.com; 148 (top left): Michael Dodge–CA/Getty Images; 153: shutterstock.com; 160–161: shutterstock.com; 171: ICC Women's World Cup Semi-Final, Australia vs. India, England, 20 July 2017 (Stu Forster/Getty Images); 181: after winning the ICC Women's World T20, Antigua, 25 November 2018 (Harry Trump–IDI/IDI via Getty Images); 182–183: shutterstock.com; 206–207: © Stuart Miller Photography; 213: ICC Women's World Twenty20 Semi-Final, Australia vs. India, Saint Lucia, 13 May 2010 (Photo by Clive Rose/Getty Images).

We gratefully acknowledge the permission granted by copyright holders to reproduce the copyright material in this book. All reasonable attempts have been made to contact the copyright holders; the publisher would be interested to hear from anyone not acknowledged here, or acknowledged incorrectly.

Colour reproduction by Splitting Image Colour Studio, Clayton VIC
Printed and bound in China by RR Donnelley

8 7 6 5 4 3 2 1   19 20 21 22 23

Ellyse Perry is managed by Josh White, CEO of Lampoon Group
lampoon.com.au

CONNECT WITH ELLYSE
FACEBOOK: @ELLYSEPERRYOFFICIAL
INSTAGRAM: @ELLYSEPERRY
TWITTER: @ELLYSEPERRY
WEB: ELLYSEPERRY.COM